D1256942

FATALISM

MARK H. BERNSTEIN

FATALISM

UNIVERSITY OF NEBRASKA PRESS

LINCOLN & LONDON

The paper in this book meets the
minimum requirements of
American National Standard for
Information Science –
Permanence of Paper for Printed
Library Materials,
ANSI Z39.48–1984.

Library of Congress Cataloging
in Publication Data
Bernstein, Mark Howard, 1948-
Fatalism / Mark H. Bernstein.
p.   cm.
Includes bibliographical references
and index.
ISBN 0-8032-1227-5 (alk. paper)
1. Fate and fatalism.
I. Title.
BJ1461.B455   1992
149'.8 – dc20   91-27879
CIP

To Matilda, Louis, Nancy, Robert, Rachel, Jonah, Jedidiah, and Knish

CONTENTS

Acknowledgments   xi

Introduction   1

ONE
What Fatalism Should Be   5

TWO
The Argument for Metaphysical Fatalism   35

THREE
Fatalism, Determinism, and Freedom
toward the Past   61

FOUR
Fatalism and Moral Responsibility   95

FIVE
Wittgensteinian Fatalism   127

Notes   145

Bibliographical Essay   151

References   155

Index   161

Beyond all reason, be a romantic anyway.

ANNIE DUNDEE

ACKNOWLEDGMENTS

I thank *Philosophical Studies* for allowing me to use "Fatalism, Tense, and Changing the Past," 56 (1989), as a substantial part of chapter 2.

I am grateful to Jacques Barzun, who supplied a historian's perspective on some issues discussed in my book.

My biggest debt is to Hector-Neri Castañeda, without whom this project never would have been begun. He convinced me, during a National Endowment for the Humanities seminar in the summer of 1984, that fatalism was not a dead issue and encouraged me to examine it in a book. He also provided Castañedan (lengthy, substantive) comments on a paper I wrote on fatalism.

Let me also express my gratitude to Bob Kane and Al Martinich, two other colleagues and friends who made significant suggestions about drafts of early chapters.

Finally, I thank Nancy Daley for her herculean efforts in transcribing the oral into the written and Laura Saucedo and Thomas J. Wood for their almost mystical ability to translate my longhand hieroglyphs into a legible typescript.

This is a work on fatalism, the thesis that whatever happens must happen. If time confers respectability on philosophical problems, there are few issues in the history of philosophy with more right to be carefully and charitably considered than fatalism. Yet in the twentieth century, at least, this approach has certainly not been adopted. Contemporary discussions of fatalism have been scattered and perfunctory, almost always concluding with a summary dismissal of the fatalist's argument. Typically the fatalist is seen as making some rather sophomoric blunder—mistaking a tautology for a substantive thesis about necessity, misunderstanding the scope of a 'modal operator', misrepresenting facts about the future as facts about the past, and the like. These characterizations, though not to be precluded a priori, should give one pause. The Stoics, Peripatetics, and other ancients such as Aristotle certainly took the problem seriously. To dismiss the opinions of these philosophers so cavalierly is presumptuous, condescending, and unfair. But what is most damaging is the harm we do to ourselves by such an attitude. We lose the opportunity to reach a better understanding of some of our basic conceptual machinery concerning such fundamental notions as time and truth.

To forestall any aberrant expectations, let me state quite forthrightly that I do not argue that fatalists have produced or can produce any obviously sound argument for their position. All arguments, including counterfatalistic ones, rely on presuppositions, and ultimately one chooses the presuppositions, and thus the argument, one finds most satisfying. Although the ultimate acceptance of presuppositions may be arational, they will on pain of incoherence commit one to a host of other positions. If one is either a fatalist or an antifatalist, one needs to accept much conceptual baggage; the choice revolves around what one wishes to keep, rather than whether to discard the luggage altogether. Indeed, it is just the articulation of these conflicting assumptions on presuppositions that I view as the main burden of chapter 2. It has never, at least to my satisfaction, been made clear just what the *antifatalist* is compelled to accept in making a rebuttal to fatalism. This is not to prejudge that this weight is intolerable or even unduly burdensome, but I do suggest that the usual portrayal of the dialectic—the antifatalist parrying every fatalistic gambit with nary a nuance of metaphysical underpinning—is simplistic and not true to the facts.

To return to the beginning, chapter 1 argues that the received—indeed virtually unanimous—view that fatalism is a logical or conceptual thesis is a caricature. Although this view is historically inaccurate, the main cause for disenchantment with it is that such an interpretation of fatalistic necessity (of the fatalist's 'must') unfairly trivializes the entire debate. If we understand the fatalist as asserting a logical or conceptual truth, the dispute quickly disintegrates into a verbal issue, with both sides hurling epithets that have little if any connection with matters philosophical. One would think—or at least hope—that two millennia of concern would amount to something more. It can and does if we view fatalistic necessity 'metaphysically', as understanding the fatalist as imputing to all events, and most significantly to future events, the same necessity we all commonsensically impute to events in the past. This type of necessity, which we need not find reducible to logical necessity, forms the basis of meaningful debate and allows us to investigate certain metaphysical notions that would otherwise go unattended.

Chapter 3 elucidates metaphysical fatalism by considering in some detail the nature of past necessity; that is, what kind of necessity is utilized by metaphysical fatalism and in what such necessity is grounded. This necessity is compared with the type implemented in traditional discussions of free will, particularly in disputes concerning the reconcilability of free will with determinism. I take advantage of this opportunity to also conduct a telescopic inquiry of the nature of the free will problem itself, an investigation independent of one's position concerning the viability of metaphysical fatalism.

Chapter 4 examines the relation between fatalism and moral responsibility. Although I argue that much of the concern about fatalism is independent of moral considerations per se, there can be little doubt that the central fear fatalism injects in the minds of most persons is that its truth would preclude any justified ascription of moral responsibility. Fatalism seems to exempt us from the category of moral agents, dehumanizing us and deflating our self-concept to the point where we must seriously question our privileged status. Healthy corrective or not, the major issue is whether this fear is legitimate or chimerical, and to this end we need to investigate the nature of moral assessment. The key moral intuition that 'ought implies can' will command a great deal of our attention.

In chapter 5 I consider Wittgenstein's views on fatalism and determinism. The source for my interpretation of Wittgenstein's remarks is the class notes of Y. Smythies (Nachlass 99) from a course he took from Wittgenstein in the early 1940s. To the best of my knowledge this is the first detailed treatment of Wittgenstein's thoughts on free will, but innovation itself does not justify including this chapter. Wittgenstein, as I understand him, has significant and original contributions to make in this problem area. Although the general tenor of his remarks may suggest a reconciliationist rendering, my reading of Wittgenstein does not have him comfortably situated in either the compatibilist or the incompatibilist camp. Whatever its historical accuracy, this understanding affords us a new perspective from which to view the fatalism debate, along with an impetus to discuss some broad metaphilosophical issues that affect our more local examination of fatalism.

Let me make some brief comments about my own approach. First, it is ahistorical. This, of course, does not mean I believe the ancients, medievals, and moderns have nothing to teach us, but only that any contributions I make to the debate will emanate from a problem-oriented viewpoint. (Readers interested in the ancient genesis and development of this issue should consult White, *Agency and Integrality*.) Second, my approach is apolemical. My aim is neither to show that some philosophers have committed terrible blunders nor to "prove" that some segment of the philosophical community has attained the final truth of the matter. Third, I have tried, as far as possible, to write a nontechnical, jargonless work. An apparent exception to this may be my frequent use of "possible world" talk. My defense is simply that this language seems to aid my own understanding of some modal issues. If it does not have this heuristic value for others, I urge them to replace it with whatever terminology they deem appropriate. In the way I utilize possible worlds, then, they do no real work, in that they do not clarify or elucidate the nature of possibility; they are no more or less than ways a situation could be. I am not interested in defending or rejecting any ontological or epistemic theories concerning such possible worlds.

ONE

WHAT FATALISM SHOULD BE

1.1 Fatalism is the thesis that whatever happens must happen. The primary task of this chapter is to provide a proper and full articulation of that thesis, which amounts to an adequate account of the fatalist's 'must'—of fatalistic necessity. This task will not be adequately discharged until the end of chapter 2, where the pivotal argument for fatalism will be discussed in detail. It is a fiction, of course, to think there must be a univocal sense of fatalistic necessity. "Fatalism" is hardly a term of ordinary usage, and so it can be defined, without serious abuse, in a number of ways. The constraints on the definition of "fatalism," on the type of necessity the fatalist employs, are pragmatic rather than conceptual. In our account of fatalistic necessity we need to maintain the apparent, if not ultimately real, conflict between it and human freedom. Since the interest in fatalism has been due to the perception that it threatens our freedom and makes us less than the full-fledged persons we normally take ourselves to be, any definition that lacks at least a whiff of this tension can be discarded as neologistic; whatever is being defined, it is not relevant to our concerns. As I will argue, however, there is one understanding of fatalistic necessity that has significant advantages over the other, more frequently voiced view. The primary advantage of my rendering of fatalistic necessity, what I deem the "metaphysical" interpretation, is that, unlike received opinion, which treats fatalistic necessity as a logical or conceptual modality, it does not trivialize the debate between fatalist and antifatalist. The principle of charity demands that we try to interpret the issue as substantively as possible, but it is more than allegiance to fairness that prompts my challenge to the received view. By adopting the metaphysical interpretation of fatalistic necessity—metaphysical fatalism—we can gain insight into that part of our conceptual machinery that deals with time and truth. A tertiary dividend is that the metaphysical interpretation seems to better reflect the actual writings and thoughts of the ancients, where of course the debate began. I realize that this consideration is double-edged; one may argue that the issue has been clarified over the course of time by advancing certain distinctions unavailable to the ancient mind. I tend not to take such a patronizing attitude. It seems to me that the intervening years have contained as much corruption as clarification.

1.2 We may call the view that identifies fatalistic necessity with logical (conceptual) necessity "logical fatalism." We can state logical fatalism in a host of equivalent ways. Indicative among them: (*a*) all events, regardless of the tense[1] of their occurrence, are logically necessitated; (*b*) if and only if an event occurs, regardless of its tense, in one logically possible world, it occurs in all logically possible worlds; (*c*) if an event occurs, in whatever tense, it logically could not fail to occur; (*d*) the actual world is the only logically possible world; and voluntaristically rendered, (*e*) it is a logical truth that the only powers we possess are instantiated ones.

One possible source of confusion should be removed immediately. The logical fatalist does not believe that event descriptions are mere tautologies or logical truths. Attending to a claim about the past, say, 'World War II occurred in the 1940s', the logical fatalist avers that neither it nor its negation is entailed by logical laws. He does not, then, claim to be able to tell merely from an event description whether or not the event so described actually obtains, let alone whether its satisfaction or lack thereof is logically necessitated. Alternatively, the logical fatalist understands 'occurring event' as a pleonasm when he claims that all events are logically necessitated. This is hardly idiosyncratic. It is, after all, rather difficult to understand what a nonoccurring (in any tense) event amounts to, just as it is difficult to understand what a nonexistent table is. In any case, all but radical Meinongians would agree that 'they' are not types of events or types of tables. The point of introducing the notion of event descriptions is that, since event descriptions may have no referents (e.g., 'the world war that occurred in the 1890s'), it demonstrates that the logical fatalist does not claim to know a priori whether some event description picks out a state of affairs in the actual world. However, he assures us that *if* it does pick out something in the actual world, it denotes a state of affairs that constitutes part of every logically possible world.

Let me begin explicating metaphysical fatalism by considering an event (or equivalently for our purposes, a state of affairs), over whose occurrence we typically (preanalytically) believe we have control. Such events are future occurrences. We believe that if we undertake certain actions, actions we are free to perform, one particular result will occur, whereas if we undertake a different set, which again we are free to perform, different consequences will ensue. Thus when we exercise certain of our abilities, the constitution of the world is different than it would be had we not done so. This commonsense attitude we have toward the future—or if you like, the natural attitude that characterizes the relation between our abilities and the constitution of future events—is aphoristically captured by the claim that the future is open.

Notice that our natural attitude toward the past is quite the reverse. We believe the past is closed, that is, that at present we have no ability to undo or modify the past to any extent. Concomitant with these attitudes toward the tenses is a belief in "time's arrow," the idea that time marches inexorably toward the future. Thus there is a sense in which, though it is now impossible to change the past, it was not always impossible, for what now constitutes the past was at one time part of an open future. Although it is beyond any person's ability to undo the atrocities of the Nazis in World War II, for example, it was presumably in Hitler's power in the 1940s to make these horrors never be part of the actual world. When we speak of the closedness of the past, then, we understand 'the past' *attributively,* as those events, whichever they may

7

be, that constitute the past at a particular time. In understanding these descriptions *referentially,* as picking out particular events at the time of utterance, our attitudes suggest alterability. That it sounds strange to say we can change the past implies that we rarely use the description referentially, and I will adhere to this common practice of attributive use throughout.

Let me emphasize that the prephilosophical beliefs toward the past and future are ontological, not epistemic. Surely we naturally believe that mistaken beliefs about the past may be corrected. Nonetheless, although our beliefs about the past may change, it remains true that the past is left unchanged; although the extent of our knowledge of the past may well be modified over time, this occurs not because the past conforms to our present beliefs, but because our beliefs come to mirror an unchangeable past.

This background provides us with a good introduction to metaphysical fatalism. This fatalism is best seen as viewing the occurrence of all events, including future events, as necessary in just the same way as we commonsensically view the occurrence of past events. It views the future as being as closed as the past; just as we now have no ability to rearrange the furniture of the past, we likewise have no power to change the content of the future. Fatalistic necessity, then, is identified by the metaphysical fatalist with the necessity of the past, whereas the logical fatalist identifies it with the necessity of logic.

We will discover presently how this difference manifests itself, but first it is worth emphasizing the important opinions these two views share. Perhaps most significant, they both deny what the person of common sense, the antifatalist, asserts—that the future's constitution is in large measure up to us. On the other hand, all three positions agree that the past is closed. The antifatalist, then—the person of common sense—is really an anti–future fatalist; his disagreement has to do only with the restrictions that the fatalist places on our ability to affect the character of the future. They share the belief that, relative to the present, the past is inviolable.

Second, both metaphysical and logical fatalists view their positions concerning the future as more than advocacy to the tautology 'whatever will be, will be'. Of course what will occur will occur, but the fatalist claims that *what* will occur—the constitution of the future—is not amenable to the exercise of any of our powers. Compare his attitude toward the future with our natural attitude toward the past, where our allegiance toward the closedness of the past goes beyond the mere tautology 'whatever has occurred, has occurred'. The "additional" component lies in our attitude that *what* has occurred—the past—is not susceptible to modification by any of our present actions.

Although fatalistic necessity has so far been characterized voluntaristically, in terms of persons' abilities or powers, note that the necessity is meant to have broader scope. The closedness of a tense, be it present, past, or future, is supposed to preclude the possibility that any part of its constitution can be altered, by personal or by impersonal means. It is quite natural, however, to restrict the discussion to personal abilities, for it is our alleged inability to affect the constitution of the future that gives fatalism its bite. The fear, after all, is that our freedom, our ability to matter in the events that constitute the world's history, is altogether vitiated by fatalism.

One might, with ecumenism of spirit, admit this fatalistic necessity but still hold that many of the properties of the event in question are to be determined by the exercise of certain of our abilities. So, for example, one might hold that World War II is fatalistically necessitated but claim that the identity of the combatants, countries, and times of the particular battles are all open. One might, that is, argue that in some broad sense of 'event' World War II is necessitated while maintaining that some, if not most, of its properties are contingent. In this way one might take fatalism as merely compromising, rather than eradicating, our freedom. But this misconstrues the global nature of fatalism. We need not worry whether and how such distinctions between an event and its properties can be made, for the fatalist's notion of necessity is ultimately fine-grained. It ascribes necessity to any future state of affairs regardless of its minuteness or relative insignificance. Just as we now can do nothing about the number of men killed in World War II or the location of the wounds that led to their deaths, the fatalist similarly assures us that we can do nothing about the particular incidents that constitute World War

9

III, let alone—if one wishes to make a distinction—prevent this future event from happening. A future event will occur, and all the properties of such an event will exist with absolute guarantee.

1.3   It is open to a logical fatalist to argue that fatalistic necessity should be identified with logical necessity and that this latter necessity has no relevant ties to the necessity of the past. On this view, it is simply a false start to try to understand fatalism as being founded upon metaphysical necessity. In practice, however, logical fatalists have accepted the metaphysical interpretation (the argument for which will be rigorously discussed in chap. 2) but have claimed that this past necessity is itself a type of logical necessity (LN), in that the belief that the past is inviolate is a belief in a logically inconsistent state of affairs. In the end, my critique of logical fatalism will apply to both strategies, but we will learn more if we continue to defer to tradition and investigate whether past necessity is logically vouchsafed.

Let us then, for the sake of concreteness, consider the past event, World War II. The logical fatalist understands the past necessity of World War II in the following way:

(LN)   In no logically possible world in which World War II occurs as part of that world's past does anyone (after the occurrence of World War II) have the power to make it the case that World War II not be a past event in that world.

That is, the suggestion is that fatalistic necessity amounts to the logical incompossibility of a past event's occurrence and the power to undo or modify that event.

The argument for understanding fatalistic necessity in accordance with logical necessity is portrayed as quite straightforward. Assume one has the power to undo a past event. Then, minimally, in one logically possible world, one brings about that event's nonoccurrence. But since the relevant subset of logically possible worlds comprises just those worlds in which the past event actually occurred, we are left with a world in which the selfsame event both occurs and does not occur at

10

some particular past time. But this is a contradictory state of affairs, which is just to say that there is no such logically possible world. Therefore the assumption that led to this impossibility must be rescinded. Thus past necessity, the necessity equated with the past's unmodifiability, is explicable in terms of logical necessity.

For the moment, let us not be concerned with the merit of this argument; for whether or not it is tempting to use this sort of reasoning to justify our belief in the necessity of the past, it is clear that any antifatalist (by whom I mean a person who advocates past fatalism while renouncing future fatalism) cannot advocate it. This is because the argument can be transported, mutatis mutandis, to demonstrate our inability to affect the constitution of the future.

To see this, consider whether there are any logically possible worlds that contain both World War III, which is a future event, an event that will occur in that world, and a person's power to make it the case that World War III does not occur. If one has the power to bring about World War III's nonoccurrence, then in some logically possible world World War III's nonoccurrence is brought about. But since we are concerned only with those worlds in which World War III will occur—that is, does occur at some future date—we are left with a world in which World War III both occurs and does not occur at some future date. But this state of affairs is inconsistent, and so there are no such logically possible worlds. That is, it is logically incompossible that World War III occur at some future time and that a person have the power to bring about its nonoccurrence. But this is just to surrender victory to the (future) fatalist.

Thus the very natural attempt to justify our belief in a closed past by appealing to the putative fact that alteration of the past is logically impossible must be resisted by the antifatalist, for as I am understanding him he advances the commonsense positions of both a closed past and an open future. He is compelled, then, to discover some flaw in this argument that tries to justify, as a mere matter of logic, the inviolability of the past. In other words, the ordinary person of common sense cannot be even a partial logical fatalist; he cannot accept the necessity of the past as a logical doctrine. We have then, surprising allies: the metaphysical fatalist who denies logical fatalism and the everyday antifatalist. The error these two strange bedfellows claim to find is a misunderstanding, by the logical fatalist, of the notion of "power." According to them, all that can be legitimately deduced is that it is logically incompossible that a future (past) event occur and that the power to bring about its nonoccurrence be *instantiated*. This, it will be granted, is indeed a logically impossible state of affairs. However, it leaves untouched both the antifatalist's claim—that the power (but not its exemplification) to bring about a future event's nonoccurrence can coexist with the event's actual occurrence—and the metaphysical fatalist's contention that it is logically possible (although of course metaphysically impossible) for the past to be modified. The antifatalist would insist that it is perfectly proper to hold that in one and the same logically possible world one may have the power to bring about a past event's nonoccurrence and yet have that past event occur, although this does not imply that the power is exercised in that particular world.

One might object that this response burdens the antifatalist's position irreparably. Since, as seems indisputable, the arguments for past and future fatalism are truly analogous, doesn't his refusal to accept the fatalist's argument for a closed future commit him to accept the possibility of an open past? That is, the objection continues, there is now no reason for the antifatalist to deny that one can coherently be an anti–past fatalist, a person who claims it is within his power to change the past. The road now seems cleared for an anti–past fatalist to claim there is a logically possible world in which he has this power, although he will be quick to admit that the power is not manifested in that world. Furthermore, in the worlds in which this power is exercised the event does not occur, but these considerations do not militate against his position any more than analogous considerations militated against the anti–future fatalist's claim that his actions are effectual toward the future.

These considerations are damaging to the antifatalist only if he insists upon conflating past necessity with logical necessity, and thus he is provided with a first incentive to search for a different understanding of past necessity. For what the logical fatalist's rejoinder shows is not that one cannot hold to both a closed past and an open future, but merely that one cannot consistently deny future fatalism, logically conceived, while maintaining past fatalism as a logical thesis. What the antifatalist needs to do is sustain his opposition against equating past necessity with logical necessity (and so relieve himself of any thought that altering the past presents a logical impossibility) while proposing empirical considerations that account for the closedness of the past. In short, the antifatalist needs to accept metaphysical fatalism for the past while rejecting any argument that this thesis extends toward the future. This once again shows that the antifatalist and the metaphysical fatalist share the same bed, albeit not for the entire night.

1.4   We now need to return to the question of the legitimacy of logical necessity as an analysis of past necessity. Our examination will lead to revelations whose significance will extend beyond this local issue.

The disagreement between the logical fatalist and his opponents can be summarized as follows. The logical fatalist believes that our inability to alter the past demonstrates the logical incompossibility of (i) a person's having the power to change the past and of (ii) a past event's being altered. The antifatalist as well as the metaphysical fatalist believes that our inability to alter the past demonstrates, at most, the logical incompossibility of (iii) the instantiation of a person's power to change the past and of (iv) a past event's being altered. How is such a dispute to be adjudicated?

Suppose the logical fatalist challenges his opponents to exercise the power they claim to have—to actually make it the case that some future event (an event that will occur, to be redundant) does not occur. Won't such an exercise inevitably be futile, since if the alleged ability is manifested, there will not be any future event? And since a "power" that cannot be exercised is not power at all, this thought experiment confirms the conceptual thesis of the logical fatalist.

Such a ploy is reminiscent of Berkeley's Master Argument for Idealism, in which he tries to demonstrate that it is a logical (conceptual) truth that all existents are conceived existents (perceived in a mind). The proof relies on the alleged inevitable futility of conceiving of an unconceived being. Since Berkeley, as is traditional, took conceivability as the criterion of logical possibility, this inconceivability showed that the only possible beings are conceived ones. Although various replies have been offered to this argument, I will rehearse only one, the strongest I know of that accepts conceivability as the test for logical possibility. The rebuttal points out that the conception of

(a)   a tree that exists if and only if it is conceived

is distinct from the conception of

(b)   a tree that exists unconceived.

That is, we have the conception of a tree with the property of being existence-dependent on the thoughts of persons, and we have the conception of a tree as having the property of being existence-independent of any persons' thoughts (including God's). Given the criterion of conceivability, it follows that existence, independent of minds, is logically possible. If Berkeley replies that this latter allegedly unconceived tree is already being conceived and so confirms rather than refutes his thesis, we might reply that all this consideration shows is that we cannot conceive of a tree without conceiving it. But this concession amounts to conceding a tautology; Berkeley needs to show that the concept (in the product sense, rather than the process sense) is logically inconsistent. But this seems an impossible task, since we do have such a concept; indeed, we have just characterized it and showed how it differed from the concept of a being whose existence depends on being perceived by a mind. In sum, we can, and indeed do, have the concept of a material object, although of course, in order to advance this concept (or any other) at a particular time, we need to be conceiving at that time.

Using this as a model, the anti–logical fatalist will reply that the inevitable futility the logical fatalist alludes to merely demonstrates that we cannot exercise a power without exercising it, but allegiance to this tautology gives us no reason to believe we cannot exercise a power that will forever be unexercised. The anti–logical fatalist may admit that the world might have been such that the only powers we possessed were powers to perform what we actually accomplished (cf. the world might have been such that the only objects in the world were existence-

14

dependent upon minds), but the considerations adduced by the logical fatalist give us no reason to think that our world is actually of this sort. But even more than this can be inferred by these anti–logical fatalists. If these arguments are correct, not only do we have no reason to believe that our world is of the sort the logical fatalist alleges, it has moreover been *proved* that logical fatalism is false. From the fact that we have the concept of having the power to perform acts that are not (ever) performed, then, given the conceivability criterion, it is logically (conceptually) possible that such powers exist. This flatly contradicts the voluntaristic rendering of logical fatalism. Indeed, although not generally recognized, the same fate awaits Berkeley's idealism, *if* we take it as a logical or conceptual thesis, as Berkeley himself did, at least insofar as the Master Argument is concerned. For merely having the concept of (b) (a tree that exists unconceived) shows the logical possibility, and thus the consistency, of the supposition of the existence of material objects.

The logical fatalist and logical Berkeleyan must claim that their opponents are confused when they speak of possessing the concepts of 'unexercised power' and 'unconceived existent', respectively. Let me suggest one avenue a logical fatalist may take. (It will be obvious that a logical Berkeleyan could adopt a similar strategy.) If it were true, as the anti–logical fatalist claims, that he has a coherent concept of an unexercised power, then he seems to have proved too much. For now nothing prevents someone from claiming he has the concept of a power to perform logically impossible acts. Naturally the person will not claim that he can (has the power to) perform an unperformable act, just as the anti–logical fatalist admits he cannot exercise a power without exercising it. But this is just a claim that the *instantiation* of the power requires that the act no longer be unperformed, just as the anti–logical fatalist holds that the actual exercise of a power requires that the power no longer be unexercised. In sum, the question is why one with an anti–logical fatalist bent could not by parity of reasoning demonstrate the obviously absurd position that one can do what one cannot do.

The temptation, of course, is to respond that a logically impossible act is not an act at all, and so there is simply nothing that can be done, for there is nothing there for the doing. But one must keep in mind that this is precisely how the logical fatalist understands an unexercised power or how a Berkeleyan understands an unconceived existent. One begins to wonder whether this confrontation with the logical fatalist is more debacle than debate, a mere quibble over the use of words.

One might suggest that this conclusion is precipitous; that the anti–logical fatalist's account of power or ability is the superior (right?) one, for only on his account can certain distinctions we frequently make actually be made. Consider the case of two men, neither of whom knows Spanish. One, we may imagine, has a brain dysfunction, whereas the other has already mastered many foreign languages. It seems perfectly reasonable to claim that the master language learner possesses what the brain-damaged person lacks—an ability to learn Spanish. Furthermore, this ability is to be cashed in, generally speaking, along conditionalist lines. Thus, if the master language learner wanted to learn Spanish and the time was available, he would learn, whereas the other man, try as he might, would never achieve such a goal. There is, then, a very significant difference between these two men that can be captured only by allowing that abilities may exist in an uninstantiated way. Fatalism, which allows only for exemplified dispositions, necessarily fails to mark this difference.

But the fatalist will admit to being at a disadvantage only if the distinctions we frequently make reflect real differences in the world. And as he has argued in his logical explication of past necessity, there can be no wedge between the ability to perform an action and the performance of that action. He need not demur against the merely empirical point that most persons do talk of abilities as though they could exist without exemplification, but this does not carry with it its own justification. The logical fatalist may even concede that his use is an aberration from ordinary language, but he claims it nevertheless is warranted. Moreover, he could point to historical precedent. Years ago persons thought they distinguished between witches and nonwitches and, somewhat more contentiously, between analytic and synthetic statements. We now know that these frequently made distinctions were bogus. Empirical investigation provided evidence of our mistake in the first example, conceptual investigation supplied the requisite evidence in the second. In this regard the logical fatalist would view our error in the use of disposition terms as akin to the latter case.

That fatalism as a logical doctrine does require some linguistic gerrymandering can be shown in a related way. Suppose we ask both parties for the conditions under which we can truly ascribe an ability to an agent. There will be at least one condition to which both parties subscribe: the actual performance of P by agent A suffices to show that A has, at the time of the performance, the ability to do P. Of course, to the antifatalist, but not to his adversary, there are other conditions under which abilities are truly ascribed. Fundamentally there will be two conditions, which jointly entail that A now has the ability to perform P:

and

(i)   A (or persons relevantly similar to A) have performed P (or P-like activities)

(ii) The current situation is relevantly similar to the past situation.

The use of "relevantly similar" is meant to have large and indefinite scope. Usually included under such a rubric will be such items as A's currently having the opportunity to perform P, A's not having suffered a disabling (let us not worry here about possible circularity) mental or physical handicap, and so on. Given that one keeps in mind the broad scope of this term, the antifatalist takes the argument whose premises are given by (i) and (ii) and whose conclusion is

(iii) A can (now) perform P

as deductive. That this is the antifatalist's attitude is confirmed in that purported counterexamples (where allegedly [i] and [ii] are satisfied and yet A cannot perform P) are typically dismissed as not genuine, by claiming that the current and past circumstances are relevantly dissimilar. Furthermore, the antifatalist will claim that the argument formed by (i), (ii), and

(iv) A now performs P

17

is inductive. Just how strong is the evidential link between the premises and (iv) is a matter of detail (in effect, a matter of the kind and degree of similarity of the past and present cases), but a gap between premises and conclusion will always remain, mirroring the gap between the ability of A to perform P and the actual performance of P by A.

The logical fatalist has a different view of the situation. Insofar and only insofar as (i) and (ii) give support to (iv) do they transmit support to (iii) (and conversely). The amount of justification we have for claiming (iii) on the basis of (i) and (ii) is identical to the justification we have for (iv) on the same basis. These considerations commit him solely to viewing both arguments as having the same status, not to what that status is.

A yet more radical general result about the logical status of arguments follows from the logical fatalist position. Deductive arguments are traditionally distinguished from inductive ones by the fact that the evidential link between their premises and conclusion is absolute; that is, it is logically necessary that if the premises are true, the conclusion is true. The evidential link in inductive arguments is not as secure—it is logically possible that the premises be true and the conclusion false. What is completely irrelevant to the logical status of such arguments— that is, to their deductiveness or inductiveness—is the actual truth-value of any of the statements employed in the argument. Consider an inductive argument (one we normally consider inductive) with true premises and a true conclusion. If logical fatalism is correct, such an argument is not truly inductive, for it is *not* logically possible that the premises be true and the conclusion false. There are no other logically possible worlds in which the premises are true and the conclusion false, for there are no other possible worlds. Indeed, we reach the startling conclusion that if this fatalism is true, all and only inductive arguments are those arguments whose premises are actually true and whose con-clusion is actually false. Thus this fatalistic characterization of the logical status of arguments makes relevant what a nonfatalist picture deemed irrelevant—the actual truth-values of the statements employed in the argument.

We can extend these results when we consider the notion of validity.

This can be seen quite directly if we hold, as is quite common, that the phrase "deductively valid argument" is redundant. This view has obvious advantages. For one, it eliminates any need to investigate the intentions of the person who advances the argument to determine whether the argument is deductive. Regardless of how such a person "means the argument," the argument is assessed as deductive if and only if it is valid. Assuming, as is traditional, that "valid" and "invalid" are mutually exclusive and mutually exhaustive terms, the conceptual fatalist equates inductive arguments with invalid ones. Thus invalid arguments, being identical to inductive arguments, will be those whose premises are (actually) true and whose conclusions are (actually) false.

There is, then, no denial that the concept of validity and many related notions undergo a drastic change of scope. But once again, this is an inevitable consequence of a theory that allows for the actual world as the only logically possible one. Any of our notions that rely on there being more than one logically possible world will be transformed, if not perverted, if logical fatalism is presumed. Although some may suggest that this is reason enough for discounting fatalism, or even for demonstrating its falsity, I find this dismissive attitude cavalier. Once again the logical fatalist is free to argue that this shows that some distinctions we have made, canonized though they may be in our everyday language, need to be modified or retracted altogether. What some antifatalists view as a fundamental problem, logical fatalists consider an illuminating insight.

If one does characterize these gyrations of the logical fatalist as a weakness, it is not a weakness shared by the metaphysical fatalist. The latter need not change the meaning of—or if you like, change our beliefs about—our logical assessments of arguments, since he does not hold that the actual world is the only logically possible one. Without this identification, the metaphysical fatalist is free to maintain our ordinary uses of "deductiveness," "inductiveness," "validity," and so on. Thus, to the extent that one views divergence from ordinary language as a vice, metaphysical fatalism accrues some advantage over its logical counterpart.

Be this as it may, when one reflects upon the nature of the disagreement with the logical fatalist, it is not surprising that the results are so gelatinous. When the dispute is seen as one where one party affirms and the other denies that a particular thesis is a logical truth, competing verbalisms are the inevitable result. Sooner or later the discussion degenerates into a name-calling contest, with each of the adversaries claiming that his definitions are "better," "more appropriate," or "more in accordance with common usage." The harangue becomes tiresome, unproductive, and only tangentially philosophical. It strikes me, therefore, as infelicitous when fatalism is defined or described in terms that will bring about this sort of debate.

Indeed, the real mystery would be not whether fatalism is true, but why, if it were a logical truth—a tautology—anyone would ever concern himself with it or expend time and effort writing about it. If for no other reason than the principle of charity, we must believe, at least at the outset, that fatalists and antifatalists have something meaningful to say. And this will be accomplished only by identifying fatalistic necessity with nonlogical necessity.

Let me be quite clear about what the metaphysical fatalist takes to be logically possible. He believes that some segment of the past, say t_1 to t_3, can (logically) be changed, so that it is no longer part of the past at t_4. The situation whose logical possibility is being envisioned is not the *relatively* amenable one in which an event can occur such that if it does occur the past would be constituted differently than had the event not occurred (cf. sec. 2.5), but rather the startling circumstance where the constitution of the past actually changes as the world marches toward the future.[2]

A cautionary note, however, should be sounded. The metaphysical fatalist believes, of course, that the past cannot be changed (if he didn't, his type of fatalism would hardly bother anyone), but that the 'cannot' is not logical. Although he is not committed to what, if anything, accounts for the necessity of the past, recent discussions of the intrinsic entropic nature of the universe harmonize well with his views. Contemporary cosmologists tell us that the universe is winding down, that energy is continually dissipating, and that such a progression is irrevocable. Many believe that these essential truths about matter and energy underlie the intrinsic future directedness of temporal processes. Yet the particulars of any physical theory need not concern the metaphysical fatalist's philosophical point, for as long as some empirical explanation for past necessity might be forthcoming, he will rest contented.

1.5 To further our understanding of metaphysical fatalism, it is instructive to compare it with the logical interpretation of fatalism in two significant and related areas—the analysis of counterfactual claims and the analysis of causal claims—for both of these have played important roles in the discussion of philosophy of freedom. Counterfactual claims are claims that are contrary to fact. They assert that some event would have occurred under the supposition that the world differed from the way it actually was; either, that is, if the world contained an event it actually failed to contain or the world lacked an event it actually had. A general schema for counterfactual (CF) claims that serves our purposes well is

(CF) had p occurred, f would have occurred,

where 'p' and 'f' are variables ranging over nonactual events (or nonactual omissions of events) and the event substituends for 'f' are temporally subsequent or simultaneous with those for 'p'.

Although philosophers have yet to devise a totally satisfying method of assessing the truth-value of counterfactuals, in a nonfatalistic world, a general consensus of theories revolves around the intuitive notion of similarity. Roughly, we are to imagine a world, as similar to ours as possible but where the condition supplied by the counterfactual's antecedent obtains, and then to determine whether, in such a world, the state of affairs described by the counterfactual's consequent obtains. Exactly how such similarities are to be measured and precisely how such determinations are to be managed are, fortunately, niceties we need not delve into. Applying this idea, which as broad grained as it stands is really not much more than an articulation of our preanalytic beliefs about counterfactuals, to the following claims (C) leads to nothing especially problematic:

(C$_i$)   If Bush were not president of the United States, he would be prime minister of Britain.

(C$_{ii}$)   If Bush were not president of the United States, he would not be a colonel in the Libyan air force.

Surely the Bush-presidentless worlds most similar to the actual one would not contain him as prime minister of Britain or have him as a Libyan colonel. Consider now:

(C$_{iii}$)   If Sacramento were not the capital of California, it would be the capital of California.

Though this is a bizarre-sounding statement one might well be justifiably puzzled about, our criterion gives us a satisfying result. In the world most like ones where Sacramento is not California's capital, Sacramento would obviously not be the capital of California. So (C$_{iii}$) should be assessed as false. But now we need to reflect on:

(C$_{iv}$)   If triangles were not to contain 180°, Caesar would not have crossed the Rubicon.

Following our directive, we are to imagine (conceive of) worlds most like ours where triangles lack 180° and determine whether, in these worlds, Caesar crosses the Rubicon. The problem is that 'triangles contain 180°' expresses a logical truth, a truth which is true in every logically possible world. Thus it appears to be logically impossible to follow our guideline—there simply are no worlds where triangles lack 180° (compare Wittgenstein's dictum that 'sometimes logic tells us what we can imagine'). This problem with C$_{iv}$, and the resolution or course of action that evolves from it, is especially important, because *all* counterfactuals, from a logical fatalistic perspective, are modeled on C$_{iv}$. That is, since the fatalist sees the actual world as the only logically possible world, any "state of affairs" described in the antecedent of a counterfactual is a logically impossible state of affairs. Thus, while on the nonfatalist view C$_i$, C$_{ii}$, and C$_{iii}$ are relatively unproblematic, the logical fatalist sees these counterfactuals and C$_{iv}$ as being of a piece; their resolution does not follow simply from the directive to consider similar worlds.

22

One might think that at least some counterfactuals whose antecedent describes a logically impossible state of affairs have a simple resolution. Consider:

(C_v)   If triangles were not to contain 180°, they would contain 180°.

It is tempting to employ the following reasoning: *whatever* a world would be like in which triangles lacked 180°, it would obviously not be a world in which triangles did contain 180°. In this way we bypass what was problematic. We need not concern ourselves with actually imagining worlds without 180° triangles, and we need not even bother with questions of similarity. In *all* worlds in which the antecedent condition obtains, the consequent condition does not, and so we should judge such counterfactual claims as false.

This temptation needs to be treated suspiciously. The major problem is that, in effect, it takes impossible worlds to be a subset of possible worlds, in that it presupposes a symmetrical way of understanding the terms 'possible world' and 'impossible world'.[3] As a possible world is just a situation that could occur, so an impossible world is just a situation that could not occur. But this language strongly suggests that they are both situations, albeit different ones, or that they are both worlds, albeit different in an important quality.

This seems to me bad metaphysics, but I do admit that a vigorous defender of such a suggestion could make a rather protracted argument that would yield inconclusive results. An apologist of the view that impossible worlds are (a species of) world would likely view fictional horses as a kind of horse (though with bizarre breeding) and imaginary ducks as a type of duck (though of quite a special sort), and these views, though distasteful to my ontological sense, are arguable, and it would be doctrinaire to pretend otherwise.

To avoid contentiousness, let us simply bracket counterfactuals with the form of (C_v) and concern ourselves with what is surely the more general and important sort for our purposes, those exemplified in (C_{iv}). The important point to note is that the logical fatalist understands all counterfactuals on the order of (C_{iv}), that is, where the antecedent implicitly contains a per impossibile clause. Resolution of the evaluation of such claims by the antifatalist should be applicable, mutatis mutandis, to all counterfactual claims viewed from a logical fatalist perspective.

Consider, as an artistic illustration, the eerie conversation between Sheppy and Death in Somerset Maugham's *Sheppy* ([50], 298–99). Death tells Sheppy a story wherein she unsuspectingly meets a merchant's servant in Baghdad. Death is surprised, for she has an appointment with the servant later that night in the somewhat distant city of Samarra. However, the merchant's servant misinterprets a gesture Death makes toward the merchant as a threat toward himself and hurriedly rides to Samarra, where he ultimately meets Death. When Sheppy, on hearing this tale, asks Death whether there is any escape from her, Death answers that there is not.

Taking this as a fatalistic (logically conceived) scenario, we should interpret the action of the merchant's servant as the only (logically) possible one. As a matter of logic, he could do no other than decide to ride there at the time he actually did. Does this mean that Death would have met the servant in Samarra *no matter what* the latter did—even, for example, had he stayed in Baghdad that evening? The question calls for a somewhat arbitrary reply. The fatalist's point is that the supposition is logically impossible; that it is a logical necessity that the servant ride to nowhere but Samarra that evening. The truth-value assessment of

> had the servant stayed in Baghdad (per logically
> impossible), he would not have met Death,

though perhaps capable of being influenced by theoretical considerations, is, from the standpoint of the fatalist's substantive view, a verbal matter. Thus, to characterize even logical fatalism as the thesis that 'whatever happens happens no matter what' belies a particular adoption of counterfactual assessment, an assessment that is neither entailed nor rejected by the fatalist's thesis.

If one adopts a fatalism based on metaphysical necessity—a past necessity not logically deducible—then all states of affairs referred to in the antecedent clause are metaphysically impossible but, in general, logically possible. The suppositional event could not occur in precisely the same sense that we now can do nothing about when World War I began or when Texas became part of the Union. Still, such a fatalist admits—indeed insists—that there are logically possible worlds in which World War I began in 1920 and worlds in which Texas's incorporation was a twentieth-century event. Thus the general directive for evaluating the truth-value of counterfactual claims can be followed, and so, unlike the view of the fatalist, who views his thesis as a conceptual truth, there are no special problems with the metaphysical fatalist's view of counterfactuals.

This, then, presents an independent theoretical advantage for the metaphysical interpretation. Like scientific theories, it garners support "from above," so to speak, from well-entrenched theories of counterfactuals, in that no ad hoc devices need be developed to deal with cases that fall outside the mainstream of counterfactual language. But one must admit that this judgment should not be overstated. First, for persons with strong intuitions concerning the evaluation of counterfactuals with logically inconsistent antecedents, the "special problem" for the logical interpretation of fatalistic necessity rapidly melts away. A similar fate for the problem awaits those who, though not entertaining strong intuitions one way or the other, simply do not believe that anything substantive depends on the resolution. They may suggest resolving such counterfactuals in one way, stipulatively, just to reach an agreement so conversation can continue unimpeded. Moreover, the thesis of logical fatalism did not introduce these deviant cases; we need not countenance this sort of fatalism to be concerned with antecedent clauses that describe logically impossible states of affairs. Thus, from a theoretical perspective, the fatalist is neither creating nor exacerbating a problem. He might, with much justice, point out that we need a solution to these problems anyhow and that once a satisfactory procedure is developed, we merely apply it to *all* counterfactuals instead of, as antifatalists have believed, to a rather select subset. And of course there is nothing sacrosanct about using the machinery of logically possible worlds to assess counterfactual talk. There is no reason, a priori, to assert that investigation of (decision from) those logically possible worlds most similar to the actual world is the best or most insightful way to analyze our counterfactual language. It may be, for all we know, that a more satisfactory approach will be developed in which the metaphysical rather than the logical view of fatalistic necessity actually produces problematic cases. All of this suggests that declarations of advantage, though currently justified, should be muted and provisional.

1.6 We turn now to a closely related subject—the relation between fatalism and causality. It has become virtual dogma that fatalism, understood as a conceptual thesis, precludes the existence of causal relationships. What is much less prevalent is argument to justify such dogma.

Fatalism, understood as a logical doctrine, tells us that our world is logically unique. Thus if e_1 causes e_2 in the actual world, e_1 causes e_2 in every logically possible world. Obviously, then, if logical fatalism is to be assessed as incompatible with causality, causal relationships will need to be of a particular sort. Although they obtain in the actual world, they must fail to obtain in some logically possible worlds; or if they do obtain in all logically possible worlds, some of these worlds must be distinct. Undoubtedly, the favored strategy of the fatalism/causality incompatibilist has been to urge the first option. (This is no surprise. Since many of these incompatibilists are determinists, accepting all causal relationships as logically necessitated would effectively lead to logical fatalism.) Now let us ask what may seem a rather odd question: How can it be that e_1 causes e_2 in the actual world and yet not be the case that e_1 causes e_2 in every possible world? How, that is, can causal relationships be contingent?

An obvious reply is that the relata, the events involved in a causal relationship, do not exist in every logically possible world, and since the existence of the events is necessary to the satisfaction of the causal relationship, causal relationships are contingent. That is, it is in the very nature of the causal relationship that the events involved exist contingently. (Note that the claim that the relata of a relationship need to exist for the relationship to obtain is not an empty assertion. Hamlet, one might argue, stands in the relationship to me of 'being thought of' and yet does not exist.) Is there any way to argue for this status of these events?

Suppose both events in the causal relationship did occur in every logically possible world, as logical fatalism would have it. What, exactly, is the insuperable difficulty that putatively follows from this supposition? Perhaps the charge is that we can no longer make sense of one state of affairs' being the cause of the other or that, even if we can make sense of thinking of these states of affairs as standing in a causal relationship, we could not, in any nonarbitrary way, assess one as the cause and the other as the effect.

On one understanding of causation—the Humean one—causation as an objective phenomenon amounts to no more than the constant conjunction of events. To deny, a priori, causal status to logically necessitated events on a regularity account is to claim that logically necessitated events cannot stand in temporal relation. This in turn amounts to the claim that logically necessitated events are eternal. After all, the logical fatalist, since all events in the actual world are logically necessitated and since the actual world is a temporal world, is committed (and agreeably so) to the commonsense view that events are connected by the relations of 'earlier than', 'later than', and 'simultaneous with'. It is true, of course, that according to the logical fatalist the temporal order could not have been different than it is, but this fact does not seem to make the world any less temporal. What is required of the incompatibilist is an argument for the claim that a world of logical (conceptual) uniqueness is a world without time or, what in this case amounts to the same thing, an argument to show that the logical fatalist is conceptually confused in believing even in the possibility that his position is correct. This, I submit, is a most formidable task.

Some incompatibilists will find all this beside the point, since this discussion assumes an account of causation they do not champion. On their view, regularity accounts of causation omit what is distinctive to causality. Causes are taken to be *efficacious* toward other events—their effects—and not merely to have certain temporal relations to them. Hume, of course, realized that the notion of power or determination was essential to the concept of cause, but he situated this necessity in the imagination of the individual, a consequence of the idiosyncratic way our minds operate. Hume notwithstanding, this incompatibilist places causal efficacy "out there," in the intersubjective world, and it is this view of causal relationships as expressing objective efficacy that such philosophers invariably find at odds with (logical) fatalism.

Whether we view causes as necessary or sufficient conditions for their effects (or, a fortiori, as both), their existence *matters* for the existence of their effects. So to view a cause as necessary is to say, in substance, that had the cause not occurred the effect would not have occurred either. Logical fatalism, by attributing logical necessity to all actual events, is taken to imply that nothing matters, that regardless of which events were to predate, postdate, or be simultaneous with a given actual event, that event would occur.

There are two compatibilist points to be made. A compatibilist might try to rebut this charge head-on by offering the following example. Consider the possibility of the existence of the Judeo-Christian God. A somewhat modified Cartesian might claim that a triangle's three-sidedness is caused by God's will and not conversely, and furthermore, that God's having the will he has and triangles' trilateralness are both necessary states of affairs. Furthermore, the modified Cartesian might argue that the assignments of 'cause' to God's willing and 'effect' to a triangle's three-sidedness are not arbitrary, since willings are just the sort of things that can cause, whereas three-sidedness is not. That is, causal efficacy is part of the nature of some items and not of others. If this example convinces, then we can have causal relations between logically necessitated events even where we concede, as the logical fatalist need not, that logically necessitated events are atemporal.

Second, and less contentiously, this incompatibilist charge should remind us of our earlier discussion of the treatment of counterfactuals in a (logically) fatalistic world. The fatalist would claim that these counterfactual "situations" ('had the cause not obtained . . .') are not possible situations at all. The incompatibilist, then, by claiming that fatalism precludes causality, is effectually committing fatalism to a *false* assignment to the counterfactuals

> had the servant stayed in Baghdad, he would not have met Death

and

> had God not willed a triangle's three-sidedness, it would not be three-sided.

But as previously pointed out, there is nothing inherent in logical fatalism that coerces this assignment any more than there is inherent in anti–logical fatalism the position that

> had triangles five sides, the United States would not be north of Mexico

need be classified as false.

The incompatibilist correctly perceives that if the servant did die, the logical fatalist is committed to his death in every logically possible world (this *is* the only logically possible world), but he pays only lip service to the logical fatalist's identical commitment to the servant's trip to Samarra—he insists on investigating what would have happened had the servant stayed in Baghdad. But from the logical fatalist's perspective the issue involves a logical inconsistency and so is not an issue at all. *If* one makes such counterfactuals false and claims that only true assignments would provide a compatibilist account of fatalism with causality, then of course an incompatibilist victory is ensured. But a more empty victory is difficult to imagine.

Does this mean that the logical fatalist can consistently claim compatibility with causality? If causation is understood counterfactually and compatibilism demands a true assignment to the counterfactual question, then of course the logical fatalist can comply. But this is a most hollow compatibilism, no more substantive than the incompatibilist victory that depended on the contrary counterfactual assessment. There is no motivation, internal to fatalism itself, that inclines a decision one way or another. Instead of thinking in terms of compatibilism or incompatibilism, it is perhaps best to view fatalism and causality as theses that pass each other by.

Let us now consider the relation between causality and fatalism where the latter is considered a metaphysical doctrine. If all events have the necessity of past events, can causal relationships obtain between our present actions and future events? The contentious point arises, as before, when we take causation as providing efficacy; for if one assumes merely a Humean model of causation—a model where causation is nothing more than constant conjunction of events—then metaphysically necessitated events can certainly compose relata of causal relationships. The notable question, given that future events have metaphysical necessity, is whether our present actions can matter or make a difference to the constitution of the future.

A fruitful approach to this issue is to look at events that paradigmatically manifest past necessity—past events—and see whether our present actions can be causally efficacious toward them. In other words, we need to discuss the validity of backward causation or retrocausation. What the retrocausationist needs to defend is that retrocauses can have the same relation to retroeffects as we normally believe (forward) causes have to (forward) effects. From the perspective of efficacy (or determination, or power), this basically amounts to a defense of the counterfactual interpretation of retrocausation—that had the retrocause not occurred, the retroeffect also would not have occurred. Let us be quite clear that the retrocausationist is *not* claiming he can change the past; he is not claiming that anyone or anything possesses a power such that its exemplification would cause a past event (an event that had actually occurred in the past) to no longer be part of that world's history. The retrocausationist's position is much more modest; he claims it is possible for a power to exist such that were it instantiated, the past would contain an event that otherwise it would not contain.

The intuition against the viability of retrocausation is strong. Assume that a particular retroeffect has occurred and then imagine the prevention of the occurrence of the alleged retrocause. Thus we have the retroeffect occurring without its putative retrocause, thus violating the counterfactual criterion for the relation between the retrocausal relata's being causal and, a fortiori, being retrocausal.

The retrocausationist may reply that although the retroeffect and retrocause are distinct metaphysical events, it might be that the identity of which events constitute the relata of the retrocausal relationship is not ascertainable until after the occurrence of an event's retrocause. On this reading, the retrocause could not be prevented because it would be impossible to discern which event was the retrocause until after it (and, a fortiori, its retroeffect) had occurred.

This response is unlikely to silence the antiretrocausationist. He would urge that his complaint is not really epistemological in character and that its solely metaphysical nature can be shown by the following thought experiment. Assume there are some events that are retroeffects of some as yet not occurring retrocause. Furthermore, let us, in compliance with the retrocausationist's point, allow that at the time after the retroeffect's occurrence but before its retrocause's occurrence, the identities of which events are the respective retrocause and retroeffect are not ascertainable. Still, we can imagine that the world is destroyed at this time, thus making impossible the occurrence of any events and so, trivially, the events that were to serve as retrocauses. Thus we need not rely on any epistemic point concerning the identification or discrimination of events *as* retrocauses or retroeffects in order to show that retrocausation would allow that effects may occur without their respective causes. But since this is not a possibility under the counterfactual criterion for causal relationships, retrocausation is not possible.

Though a powerful objection, it is still, I believe, inconclusive. A first retrocausationist response might be to claim that although retrocauses must postdate their effects, it may just be that all retrocausal relationships are temporally dense or temporally contiguous. Under this supposition, there would literally be no time at which some intervening event could occur. This response is not to be conflated with making the causes and effects simultaneous, for this would no longer be, definitionally, a case of retrocausation. A second line of defense would allow that in at least some retrocausal relationships a temporal gap does separate the retroeffect from its cause but would claim that where this gap exists the nature of the retroeffect requires the existence of its retrocause. That is, given the way the world works—the empirical laws of nature—the occurrence of the retroeffect determines the existence of its respective cause and so mandates that no interfering event occurs. If the antiretrocausationist counters that these responses demonstrate the vacuity of his opponent's position, that what his opponent labels "retroeffects" and "retrocauses" are no more than ordinary causes and effects, the retrocausationist can point out that he is implementing the same counterfactual criterion as his adversary in demarcating causes and effects; that is, had the logical possibility that the retrocause not occur obtained, the retroeffect would not have occurred. The antiretrocausationist's charge that "successful" retrocausation merely amounts to ordinary causation with terminological change can be met in kind by the retrocausationist, who can with equal justification claim that "successful" ordinary causation is retrocausation in a different linguistic guise.

Briefly, let us consider another prime attack on the viability of retrocausation, the claim that retrocausation is compatible with the existence of causal loops and so is not possible. The objection relies on the notion that one event cannot be both the cause and the effect of some other particular event. Yet if some event e_1 retrocauses some prior event e_2, what is to prevent e_2 from causing some subsequent event e_3, which in turn causes e_1? Transitivity of causation leaves us with e_1 as both cause and effect of e_2. (Indeed, we could leave out e_3 altogether, thereby sparing ourselves possible problems concerning transitivity.) We can conceive of a retrocausationist's reply by heeding the strategy he employed earlier. It may eventuate that retrocaused events cannot produce certain effects. Thus it may be a brute fact about the world (about matter, energy, causation, and time) that those events that have subsequent causes cannot have any causal effect, direct or indirect, on those causes.

If this mode of argument is persuasive and retrocausation is a viable phenomenon, to be understood just like forward causation except that the causes and effects are temporally interchanged, there appears to be no additional reason to believe that fatalism, metaphysically understood, is incompatible with causality. On the other hand, one might still be unhappy countenancing retrocausation and allowing for the compatibility of (future) fatalism with (forward) causation. If one thought that the problem of causal loops still remained as a formidable obstacle to retrocausation, one could give up retrocausation but maintain the compatibility of ordinary causation with metaphysically necessitated future events. Since the events so necessitated are subsequent to one's present actions, worries about occurrences' being mutually causes and effects would not materialize. Moreover, the concern epitomized in the "destruction scenario" would no longer apply to the metaphysical necessitation of future events. Since the cause would occur before the effect, just as in ordinary nonmetaphysically necessitated cases of forward causation, there would never be any time after the effect but before its cause in which to set off the world's destruction. The incompatibilist's case is reduced to the thought that if an event is metaphysically necessitated, no prior event can enjoy efficacy toward that event. This is simply the same issue that has already been discussed in connection with the analysis of counterfactual claims in a metaphysically necessitated universe.

1.7   I have gone to some lengths to contrast the received view of fatalism's status—that it is a logical or conceptual thesis—with the interpretation that takes fatalism as a metaphysical thesis. I have argued that once the contrast is illuminated, serious advantages appear in adopting the latter perspective. Nevertheless, perverse as it may now seem, as far as the impact on the issue of freedom is concerned, the difference between the logical and metaphysical views is minimal. Since logical necessity entails past necessity, but not conversely, one could grant the truth of metaphysical fatalism yet hold that persons are free because it is logically possible for them to act otherwise. The question then arises whether this is freedom in the "relevant sense"; does freedom, so understood, supply us with enough "elbow room" (to appropriate Dennett's picturesque phrase) to ground the picture we have of ourselves as dignified human agents? In my view it does not. I do not derive great solace from hearing that though World War III's occurrence is guaranteed in precisely the same manner and degree as World War II's, it is logically possible that World War III is preventable. If all my future actions have this status, my lack of freedom and dignity is hardly mitigated by the reminder that these future acts need not logically occur. My speculation is that this is unfreedom enough for all of us.

This being the case, it is most unlikely that a licit form of freedom will intrude if fatalism is viewed as a logical thesis. The problem with adopting this latter view, rather, lies in its enticement to trivialize and mischaracterize the debate and, consequently, induce us to neglect issues of time and truth that should be deemed essential to the disputants' cases. Let us turn now to an investigation of the key argument for fatalism to see how these issues arise.

THE ARGUMENT FOR METAPHYSICAL

FATALISM

2.1 There are certain presuppositions that I will take the fatalist and antifatalist to share. These assumptions deal with some basic claims concerning the intimately related categories of propositions, truth, and time. The existence of such entities will be considered common background, although their precise nature will loom as a significant point of disagreement. By assuming the existence of propositions, I will be assuming that there are truth bearers—objects amenable to predications of truth and falsity. Whether such propositions ought to be identified with sentences, utterances, thoughts, or something else entirely is not crucial for our purposes. Also, we may forgo discussing whether propositions are abstract or concrete, universal or particular. If at times a mode of speech seems to imply a commitment to a particular ontology, let it be understood that such a connection is accidental, that verbal maneuvering could extinguish any appearance of essential connection.

Truth and falsity are assumed to be properties of propositions. In our unphilosophical moments, only the most argumentive would aver that they do not know what it means for a proposition to be true (or false). Nonetheless, as a means of supplying some elucidation, I submit Aristotle's comment from the *Metaphysics,* with which few of us would disagree: "To say of what is that it is not, or of what is not that it is, is false, while to say of what is that it is, and of what is not that it is not, is true."

To say that time exists is to make the minimal claim that some temporal propositions are literally true. So understood, only diehard Parmenideans and McTaggartians are likely to demur, and though their arguments are worthy of study, we will not be concerned with them here.

We come now to various theses whose mutual acceptance has proved problematic: the principle of bivalence (PB), the law of excluded middle (LEM), and in the Tarskian spirit, a very weak and restricted thesis schema for truth (RT).[1] I am cognizant that various philosophers have thought that the sole way to thwart fatalism's argument is to deny at least one of these rather commonsense ideas, ideas whose nontechnical expression might well be considered platitudes. I refuse to take this route for four reasons: it tends to be ad hoc; it is a relatively unenlightening method of trying to disarm fatalism, since it encourages us not to look at the depth of the fatalist's argument and our possible responses to such argument; it seems to discard baby and bathwater together; and there are other more profound and less costly avenues of reply.

PB states that every proposition is either true or false, where a false proposition is merely the denial of a true proposition. The statement of LEM is not unequivocal. Some authors make no distinction between PB and LEM. Others take LEM as the claim that the disjunction formed by a proposition and its denial is true. In fact, once we accept

(RT)   'p' is true if and only if p,

where 'p' is a variable ranging over propositions, the difference between PB and LEM loses significance, since the latter can be derived from the former with the aid of one classical assumption.[2] Since nothing of import in my discussion results from the distinction between PB and LEM, I will employ the more familiar LEM terminology.

To be fair, there are some problems in quantum physics and pure mathematics that seem to demand the drastic step of resigning LEM. Some scientists take Heisenberg's Uncertainty Principle as demonstrating that an electron with a specific position neither has nor lacks any particular momentum. Also, some mathematicians see LEM as violated when speaking of the Continuum Hypothesis. Arguendo, let us grant these as legitimate exceptions. Still, it is difficult to see how such obviously esoteric examples lend credence to LEM's being inapplicable to propositions concerning the most mundane subject matter discussed in the most ordinary way. One might respond that by admitting such exceptions, the onus of truth shifts to the apologist of LEM; it is now up to him to provide positive arguments for the acceptance of even its limited viability. My suspicion is that no such arguments will or can be forthcoming, that the soundness of any such argument will be more dubious than the conclusion it tries to reach. Whether this shows that the request for such arguments is illegitimate or that our paradigmatic conceptual apparatus must employ LEM is a metaphilosophical issue that is, fortunately, tangential to our major concern. We will see how well the antifatalist fares "encumbered" with this traditional principle of thought.

With RT, our commonly presupposed ontology inherits the entrance of facts or states of affairs. Facts, those entities supplied by the right side of the equivalence, are what make propositions true; or equivalently, propositions have the truth-value they have by virtue of certain facts. We know what facts "correspond" to which propositions by using the principle of disquotation. It is true, of course, that RT by itself gives no reason to believe in a dependence relation between propositions and facts. Moreover, even when we introduce this relationship as being implied by RT, there is no reason facts should depend on the truth of propositions as propositions; truth-values depend on facts. None but the most radically idealistic find this asymmetric relationship puzzling. Surely Aristotle, once again, correctly describes our conceptual framework when, in the *Metaphysics*, he says: "It is not because we think truly that you are white that you *are* white, but because you are white that we who say this have the truth."

Accepting RT, as we will understand it, has the additional benefit of being congenial to our natural way of speaking. We slide easily between talking about propositions' being true and facts' (states of affairs) obtaining. If facts just are those entities that account for the truth of propositions, the accuracy of this common mode of speech gains some theoretical support.

With this stage setting, we are now prepared to discuss the fatalistic thesis. My strategy will be to set out and discuss a traditional and representative argument for fatalism portrayed in two guises, RF and RF′. (I use 'RF' to stand for 'representative fatalism'.) In deference to Aristotle, I will use as a representative token of a future contingent proposition (a proposition that corresponds to a state of affairs we believe, prephilosophically at least, need not happen), 'there will be a sea battle on 1/1/95'. I do not claim that this argument is representative of all fatalist arguments, and so not all that is said concerning RF and RF′ will be transportable, mutatis mutandis, to other fatalistic ploys. Nonetheless, both these versions are typical of most fatalistic thinking, have historical precedent at least as remote as Diodorus Cronus, and unadornedly capture, better than all other attempts, the kernel of plausibility that draws the interest and attention of philosophers and nonphilosophers alike. Last, these guises, unlike many of their companions, allow for fruitful and penetrating discussion of the nature of propositions, truth, and time.

2.2

(RF)   (i)   'There will be a sea battle on 1/1/95' is true, or 'there will not be a sea battle on 1/1/95' is true.

       (ii)   If 'there will be a sea battle on 1/1/95' is true, then there will be a sea battle 1/1/95; if 'there will not be a sea battle on 1/1/95' is true, then there will not be a sea battle on 1/1/95.

      (iii)   If there will be a sea battle on 1/1/95, then it was always a fact that there will be a sea battle on 1/1/95; if there will not be a sea battle on 1/1/95, then it was always a fact that there will not be a sea battle on 1/1/95.

      (iv)   If it was always a fact that there will be a sea battle on 1/1/95, then there is nothing that could ever be done to prevent the sea battle; if it was always true that there will not be a sea battle on 1/1/95, then there is nothing that could ever be done to bring about the sea battle.

(v)   Thus, if 'there will be a sea battle on 1/1/95' is true, there is nothing that could be done to prevent it; if 'there will not be a sea battle on 1/1/95' is true, there is nothing that could be done to bring it about.

(vi) Either nothing could prevent the sea battle from occurring on 1/1/95, or nothing could bring about the sea battle's occurring on 1/1/95.

(vii) Generalizing, whatever happens must happen, and whatever fails to happen cannot happen.

(RF') is constructed from (RF) by replacing (ii) and (iii) with (ii') and (iii').

(ii') If 'there will be a sea battle on 1/1/95' is true, then 'there will be a sea battle on 1/1/95' was always true; if 'there will not be a sea battle on 1/1/95' is true, then 'there will not be a sea battle on 1/1/95' was always true.

(iii') If 'there will be a sea battle on 1/1/95' was always true, then it was always a fact that there will be a sea battle on 1/1/95; if 'there will not be a sea battle on 1/1/95' was always true, then it was always a fact that there will not be a sea battle on 1/1/95.

It is instructive to compare these two arguments. In RF, (ii) seems to make straightforward use of RT, and (iii) introduces the notion of a tensed (or temporal) fact, by which I mean the concept of a fact's obtaining at a particular time. In contrast, RF makes no such straightforward use of RT, but rather in (ii') introduces the notion of tensed (or temporal) truth, by which I mean the concept of a proposition's being truth-valued at a particular time. In (iii'), the notion of tensed facts is incorporated, and a connection between tensed truth and tensed facts is exploited. We will find that the basic line of thought that fuels the plausibility of RF serves a similar function for RF', and so at root the arguments are very much the same. It would be a queer fatalist indeed who embraced one while rejecting the other.

Before launching into a somewhat detailed examination of tensed propositions and facts, it is worthwhile to gain some overall perspective on why the issue appears to have nuclear significance. Premise (iv), which remains constant in both RF and RF', receives its plausibility from our belief that the past is inviolate—that nothing can be done to modify the past in any way. If, however, it is illegitimate to employ the notion of tensed facts and tensed propositions, then (iv) and the fatalistic machinery used to reach (iv), in the form of (i–iii) and (i'–iii'), would be verboten. If the only viable ways to speak of propositions and facts were atemporal or tenseless, then we would never find ourselves in a position where our commonsense belief about the past might logically coerce us into abdicating our equally commonsense belief about the openness of the future. Traditionally, the major battle has been fought over just this issue, and although I will describe some maneuvers that can be utilized even if one concedes the issue of tense to the fatalist, it seems evident that the temporalization of propositions and facts is necessary for any representative argument he may use.

2.3   As is common, I equate the notions of temporal and tensed truth. There is no harm in this as long as one does not take the notion of tense to refer to a linguistic view or thesis about truth. Tenses, as commonly used in discussions in philosophy of time, are, exhaustively, the past, present, and future. Although it is obvious that we use language to talk about tenses, it is far from evident—indeed, it seems plainly false—that tense is (purely) a linguistic matter. At the very least, this idealistically oriented view should not be assumed at the outset. So to say that the Yankees won the World Series in 1927 is to talk about a tense (the past) by the use of a linguistic device (the past tense 'won'). Normally we indicate which tense we are speaking about by the tensed language we use; however, in the quasi-stipulative way most philosophers use 'tense', we need to view this relationship as merely contingent.

Temporal truth, tensed truth, is properly distinguished from atemporal (tenseless, nontemporal) truth, the view that truth has no temporal parameters, that it is "outside of time." One must exercise some caution, for the atemporal view of truth does not preclude that truth be about time, that the *content* of the truth have temporal specifications. We may mark this difference by speaking of internal versus external temporal specifications of truth. The atemporal view of truth allows for internal temporal references but not for external references. The temporal view of truth allows for (claims that it is sensible to speak about) both.

Consider the proposition

(P)   Wittgenstein wrote notes two days before he died.

Here the internal temporal reference deals with an action that Wittgenstein performed two days before his death. Neither the tensed nor the tenseless view denies the sensefulness of this proposition. The external temporal reference of P is the time(s) at which P is true, that is, the internal time of the second-order proposition

(P′)   P is true at time(s) t.

The tensed view of truth is committed to the meaningfulness of P; the tenseless view of truth is committed to its senselessness. (If talk of 'senselessness' jars your philosophical sensibilities, the term may be replaced by 'necessary falsity'.)

Already a logical advantage may be discerned by the atemporalist, for it appears that the temporalist is committed to an infinite regress. For since P is a proposition, it too is amenable to temporal predication; that is, the external temporal reference of P is the time(s) at which P′ is true, the internal time of the third-order proposition

(P″)   P′ is true at time(s) t.

Obviously this strategy is indefinitely iterable.

The temporalist, though, can be pacific about this regress, for it is innocuous. This is clear when we realize that the truth of a higher-order proposition is not required for the truth of any lower-order one. Indeed, an isomorphic regress is generated if we neglect the temporal parameters altogether. Consider proposition Q (it is neutral whether Q itself has temporal references). Even the atemporalist, we can assume, accedes to

(Q′)   It is true that Q

(Q″)   It is true that Q′

and so on. We again are faced with an infinite number of truths. Thus even if the regress were vicious, no advantage could be claimed by either party on grounds of ontological parsimony.

I have been hesitant to identify the tenseless or atemporal view of truth with the suggestion that truths are eternal, and for this I owe some explanation. I am hesitant because 'eternal' has been used in various ways. In one sense 'eternality' and 'atemporality' are synonymous. Obviously, in this sense identification is not a problem. Let us refer to this sense of 'eternal', in which an eternal entity necessarily neither contains nor instantiates a temporal element, as 'eternal$_A$'. If we wish, we can classify an attempt to temporalize such an entity as a "category mistake," to use Ryle's phrase, and classify any claim that purports to state or describe such a relationship as 'senseless' or 'necessarily false'.

Another sense of 'eternal' is 'omnitemporal'. Here an entity does not exist "outside" time but rather exists in time forever. Alternatively put, an 'eternal$_O$' entity is one that exists from the beginning to the end of time, throughout time's existence. It does not follow from this account that if a proposition has a particular truth-value at a given time it has that same truth-value at all times. If we assume that a proposition is omnitemporally truth-valued, all we can infer is that there is no moment in time when the proposition is neither true nor false. If a proposition were to change truth-values, this change would occur in time (it would be true to say, e.g., that the proposition was true at time t_1 and false at some later time t_2), although there would be no time at which the proposition was neither true nor false (i.e., truth-valued). To hold that changes occur in time does not commit one to the view that changes take time, that they have temporal duration; a change from truth to falsity may be instantaneous. That changes occur in time helps us better understand why eternal$_A$ entities cannot change. It is not as though an eternally$_A$ truthed proposition remains (temporally) true, for this picture wrongly implies a temporal element where, ex hypothesi, there is none. A better explanation would be that external$_A$ truths cannot change for the same reason that planar objects cannot have depth—a dimension necessary for the accomplishment is necessarily excluded.

In passing I should mention a third use of 'eternal', which says of an eternal entity that it is related to time as a whole is related to its successive parts. Here the 'eternal$_T$' is to be identified with the temporal process as a whole; the eternal is all of time. This whole temporal process does not occur in time; rather, conversely, time—temporal events—exists in and constitutes the process. Time is, as J. S. Mac-Kenzie says, "simply the aspect of successiveness which the eternal process contains" ([46], 404). Thus, to claim that the truth-value of a proposition is eternal$_T$ is to deny that it exists in time (in which it agrees with the eternal$_A$ conception but disagrees with the eternal$_O$ conception), but it is to accept that it is not independent of time (in which it disagrees with the eternal$_A$ conception and agrees with the eternal$_O$ conception). It is, then, in a sense, a compromise position, where the eternal does not obtain either "in" or "outside" time but constitutes it. Different though they are, eternal$_A$ and eternal$_T$ entities share the important property of unchangeability, since both views certify that a necessary condition for change, existence in time, is lacking.

The fatalist is an omnitemporalist (or eternal$_O$ theorist), but of the special sort that precludes propositions' changing their truth-values or facts' altering their 'obtaining status'. That is, if a proposition is true (false) at any time, it is true (false) at all times, and if a fact obtains (fails to obtain) at any time, it obtains (fails to obtain) at all times. The proposition-omnitemporalism is made evident in the fatalist's argument for (ii') and the fact-omnitemporalism is made evident in his argument for (iii). These arguments will be considered presently, but what is of significance at this juncture is how this position differs from the atemporalist or nonfatalist qua atemporalist. Both the temporalist and the atemporalist may express their positions as 'propositions cannot change truth values' and 'facts cannot change their obtaining status', which may lull the unwary into believing that the differences between the two camps are minimal. But this belief would be a gross error. The atemporalist's claim is based on his atemporal view of the nature of propositions and facts; their unchangeability is based on the idea that these entities exist "outside time" and so a parameter necessary for change is lacking. The temporalist's claim, on the other hand, must rely on some other fundamental beliefs we hold about the nature of propositions and facts, for according to him the temporal dimension, one sine qua non of change, is inherent in the existence of propositions and facts.

What, then, are the fatalist's reasons for his omnitemporalism? Why, in other words, does the fatalist accept (ii') and (iii)? Typically the appeal to the dubious consists of giving examples where change of truth-value or "obtaining status" seems evidently absurd. Surely if it is now a fact that the earth is round, it was a fact one thousand years ago and will be a fact one thousand years from now. Conversely, if it is now not a fact that the earth is round, it never was, nor will it ever be, a fact that the earth is round. The same point can be made from the perspective of propositions. If the proposition 'the earth is round' is now true, then at any past or future time that proposition (which of course may not be expressed by the same sentence) is true.

Ironically, the fatalist may garner additional support by adopting a scenario from a strident adversary, Peter van Inwagen. Suppose that at $time_1$ I believe I am about to die, and at some later time, t_2, I believe I am about to die. Then, to the temporalist, if what I believed was the selfsame proposition on both occasions, then at t_1 the proposition was false (for I was not about to die at t_1) and at t_2 the very same proposition became true (that is, we can assume that at the time of this belief I am about to die).

> But if that were right, I could say on the later occasion, "When I thought I was about to die twenty years ago I was *then* wrong. But what I then believed has now become true. When I look at my diary of twenty years ago and see the words 'I am about to die,' I am comforted in my present affliction by the thought that what I wrote has become true and that in consequence, nothing said in my diary is *now* false." And this would be an absurd thing to say. ([79], 32–33)

The temporalist would quite agree that the scenario is absurd but would consider this further confirmation of his theory. For the absurdity, according to the temporalist, is derived not from his tensing propositions (as van Inwagen apparently believes), but solely from the changing of propositions' truth-values. We must, as van Inwagen and others do not, separate these two positions; adherence to the former does not necessitate adherence to the latter. To fortify this claim, consider a case where what I believe on two occasions is false. Parroting the example above, we have:

> When I thought I was about to die twenty years ago, I was then wrong. What I then believed has remained false. When I look at my diary of twenty years ago and see the words "I am about to die," I am discomforted in my present health by the thought that what I wrote has remained false and that in consequence nothing said in my diary is now true.

This scenario does not appear absurd, at least not in the putatively obvious manner in which it was formerly manifested. This provides evidence for the fatalist's claim that the absurdity lies in the change of truth-value and not in tensing truth per se, since the latter operation occurs in both examples.

But it is just this distinction, which the fatalist rightly stresses, that shows that all the considerations so far adduced are considerations against changeability of truth-values and "obtainment statuses" and not for the tensing of truths and facts. We have yet to discover whether it makes sense, and if so what sense, to speak of truths and facts at times. This search will have to await one further development, for the concept of tensing truth and facts is even more deeply entrenched in the fatalist's argument than the superficial appearance of such arguments suggests. Whereas there is in RF first overt reference to tense in (iii), and in RF′ first explicit reference in (ii′), the fatalist, as he implies in his reasoning for both (iii) and (ii′), relies on a tensed version of both RT and LEM. If this diagnosis is correct, it shows that defenses of antifatalism that rely on jettisoning either LEM or RT are, in addition to being drastic exercises, overlooking an important point: the fatalist is employing a bastardized version of these truisms.

Limiting ourselves to the first conjunct of (iii) for the sake of simplicity, we find the first explicit use of tensed facts in the consequent of the conditional. But—and this is confirmed by the fatalist's discussion of (iii)—the notion of a tensed fact is implicit in the antecedent as well; that is, the first conjunct is really elliptical for 'if it is now a fact that there will be a sea battle on 1/1/95'. Now what licenses the introduction of this tensed fact? It must have been derived from a tensed reading of the antecedent (of the first conjunct, of course) of (ii), that is, " 'there will be a sea battle tomorrow' is true" is to be understood as " 'there will be a sea battle tomorrow' is now true." Thus, what the fatalist relies on is not so much

    (RT)   'p' is true if and only if p

but rather a tensed version of RT,

    (RT*)   'p' is true at t_0 if and only if p at t_0.

The transition from tensed truth to tensed fact is carried out in accordance with RT*. We can, if we wish, push the question of temporality back one final step. For surely if the fatalist understands the antecedent of (ii) as tensed, he must understand (i), and indeed the law of excluded middle, of which (i) is an instance, as having a temporal parameter. Thus the fatalist understands

    (LEM)   'p' is true or 'not-p' is true
as
    (LEM*)   'p' is true at t_0 or 'not-p' is true at t_0.

This point becomes enhanced by considering RF'. Here (ii') explicitly uses the notion of tensing truth and does so without any mention of tensed facts. It seems evident that whatever plausibility (ii') has as encountered in the fatalist's reasoning derives from taking the 'is' in 'is true' as a tensed notion, to mean 'is now'. If we understand the 'is' as tenseless—as atemporal, or completely without temporal dimension—what is expressed by either conditional in (ii') would not make sense, let alone be true. (This holds as well for [ii] and [iii] in RF.) But as before, the onset of temporality, if it is not to be ex nihilo, is derived from a tensed variant of LEM, that is, LEM*. Finally, (iii') relies once again on RT*, which permits the transition from tensed truths to tensed facts.

    The fatalist, then, is profoundly committed to what we may call the "temporal theory of propositions and facts" (TTPF), constituted by the following three statements:

(a) Necessarily, propositions are true (false) temporally (i.e., propositions have an external temporal parameter).

(b) Necessarily, facts obtain (exist) temporally (i.e., facts have an external temporal parameter).

(c) Necessarily, propositions have the truth-value they have in virtue of the obtaining of facts. The constitution of such facts is given by RT*.

We now need inquire about the legitimacy of tensing propositions and facts.

2.4 Our examination of the sensefulness of tensed propositions and facts begins by considering A. J. Ayer's deservedly famous "Fatalism" ([2]), in which he claims that "the truth of a statement [proposition] is not a proper subject of temporal predicates." He asks us to reflect on the obvious fact that the Labour party will come to power in Britain within the next three years or it will not. But certainly it is a strange question to ask whether, if it will, it is already true that it will. The oddity of this question is explicable, according to Ayer, by realizing that the question presupposes that the truth of a statement is a proper subject of temporal predication. Once we realize the foolishness of such a presupposition, the temptation to ask such a question, and concomitantly the strangeness of such a question, will vanish.

The fatalist, or temporalist qua fatalist, may admit this question is "strange," but he would not attribute this strangeness to an illicit form of predication. Rather, it is strange because the answer is obvious, for if it is true that the Labour party will come to power within three years, then it is omnitemporally true, and so trivially it is already true. In fact, allegiance to Ayer's diagnosis of the oddity's source may result in precipitous dismissals of substantive problems. Consider a situation where two persons are engaged in philosophical discussion and one, knowing full well that chairs exist, asks whether they *really* exist. This may sound queer, but it is, we may suppose, a question concerning ontological reduction. If his friend explains the oddness of the question, and thereby dismisses it, by replying that the question presupposes that theoretical entities can properly be said to exist, we would justifiably find his claim question-begging. These tactics hardly solve a perplexing issue; they dogmatically prevent one from arising.

A second Ayerian argument takes an analogical form. Just as it is senseless to speak of a second dimension of time (a time, or metatime, at which a time occurs), so too it is senseless to speak of a time at which a proposition is true. Although some would claim that a second temporal dimension does make sense, we need not cavil, for the success of the analogy is dubious. Even if temporalizing time makes no sense (we cannot meaningfully ask for the date of a date), it is difficult to discern what relevance this has to the fatalist who wishes to temporalize truths and facts. If the tensing the fatalist employs required a tensing of time, then Ayer would have made at least a prima facie point. We would then be subject to discussing whether Ayer's unargued contention against time temporalization is justified. But since the fatalist requires this notion in neither RF nor RF', Ayer's argument seems misguided.

Some argue that truth should not be tensed in order to save our logic from complications. It is true that by demanding external temporal predication, our principles of inference—much more than our rules of implication—would become more complex. The fatalist, however, might respond that this is a small price to pay for more accurate, in the sense of more fine-grained, inference rules. Furthermore, this pragmatic argument against tensed truths actually presupposes the logical point that the fatalist avows—that tensing propositions and facts is a legitimate operation.

Turning now to customary positive arguments that can be mustered to support temporalism, we begin with the fatalist who believes that his tensed view is derivable, quite directly, from facts about the English language.

The verbs 'is', 'obtains', 'exists', and the like are present-tense verbs and so are really elliptical for 'is now', 'obtains now', and 'exists now'. Thus, for example, in (i) we are really speaking, in an abbreviated way, about propositions that are now true, and in (ii) about propositions that refer to a fact that now obtains or now exists (the phrase 'which obtains [exists]', not being appended to either 'there will be a sea battle tomorrow' or 'there will not be a sea battle tomorrow', to alleviate redundancy). Thus the tensing of truths and facts, the validation of TTPF, is a consequence of our ordinary linguistic conventions.

The quickest way to deal with this ploy is to admit it. That is, the antifatalist may grant that the words 'is', 'obtains', and so forth have their present-tense implications but then coin such new words as 'sh-is' and 'sh-obtains', neologisms that have the same content as their counterparts but for which it is left an open question whether they carry tensed implications. So (i), for example, becomes

(i-sh)   'There will be a sea battle tomorrow' sh-is true, or 'there will not be a sea battle tomorrow' sh-is true.

Now we can start the debate anew. The query now becomes whether, when we claim that a proposition sh-is true, we can be taken as legitimately ascribing a tensed truth-value to the proposition. This strategy confirms what we already should have known: if the question of tensed propositions and facts is a substantive question, etymological gerrymandering will not help us. We might as well drop the offensive coinages and continue the debate in our more familiar idiom.

A second, more powerful, suggestion is that tensed propositions and facts reflect a fundamental way we conceive of these entities. This mirroring is manifest in our ordinary language. Examples are not difficult to manufacture. We do say 'what he said this morning [that the 1927 Yankees were the greatest baseball team in history] was true', 'what he said yesterday [that jazz is the most popular music] was true five years ago, but is no longer true today', and 'what he uttered [that Shakespeare is read more than Faulkner] is true now, and will remain true forever'.

Note that these same data suggest that propositions can and do change their truth-values, and concomitantly, that facts can and do alter the status of their obtainments. Since the fatalist, as well as his adversary, rejects these possibilities, it might be thought that such data are eo ipso useless to the fatalist's cause. But such a curt dismissal would be unfair since, as I noted before, tense and changeability are not mutually dependent. Though atemporality entails changelessness, the converse does not hold.

It is incumbent on the antifatalist to do one of two things: (i) claim that these ordinary pronouncements are actually meaningless, that is, pure gibberish, or (ii) admit the sense and use of such pronouncements but explain them in such a way as to show that, contrary to superficial appearances, such claims do not require an ontology of tensed propositions and facts. It seems that (i) is a virtually hopeless chore, a task that will inevitably lead to accusations of question-begging about what is to be considered meaningless (cf. the lack of success of the logical positivists in their different attempts at producing a universally accepted criterion of meaning). Thus we need to try (ii).

Consider a concrete datum, the ordinary-language sentence

> (JM)   What he said yesterday [that jazz is the most popular music] was true five years ago, but is no longer true today.

Here the parenthetical expression gives the content of what he said yesterday. We can assume that this content was given when the speaker expressed the proposition that jazz is the most popular music by uttering the sentence 'jazz is the most popular music'. Thus we have

> (JM')   'Jazz is the most popular music' was true five years ago, but is no longer true today.

The antifatalist's interpretation of JM' tells us that a *name* of a proposition was used five years ago to express a true proposition, and the same name is used today to express a different, and false, proposition. Or to put the point somewhat differently, the ordered string of words used to constitute the sentence 'jazz is the most popular music' was used five years ago to express a true proposition but is now used to express a false one.[3] Thus explicated, no threat from appeals to ordinary language is posed to the antifatalist's treatment of propositions. The sentence, uttered five years ago, expressed a proposition that is (atemporally) true, whereas the same sentence (or same name of the proposition) uttered today expresses a different proposition that also is (atemporally) false.

One might try to argue for the existence of tensed truth and facts by relying on two moderately uncontroversial theses: (a) knowledge is temporal, and (b) knowledge implies truth. In defense of (a), it certainly appears evident that human beings, if not deities, acquire and lose knowledge at certain times. One may gain knowledge of a state capital in grade school, maintain this knowledge for several years, and then lose it. Thesis (b) is only shorthand for a condition that all but invariably appears in any analysis of propositional knowledge: if A knows that p, it is true that p. Given these mutually held (let us assume) presumptions, the atemporalist is challenged to give an account of how knowledge, a relationship that takes place in time, can occur when one relatum (the proposition) exists atemporally.

Replies to this puzzle may reach various depths. Concerning ordinary empirical contingent propositions, the air of paradox may be dissolved by concentrating on the distinction between internal and external temporal predication. If, for example, one knows at 11 A.M. that the barn is red, the atemporalist will admit that, most typically, the 'is' is a present-tense verb used to signify the present tense. But one should not infer from this that it is true now (at 11 A.M.) that the barn is red, but only that

> it is [atemporally] true that the barn is [at 11 A.M.] red.

Thus the proposition has an implicit internal temporal reference that permits the hookup with one's knowledge.

Admittedly, this strategy does not transport well to cases concerning noncontingent a priori claims. If one knows that two plus two equals four, the atemporalist will take the present-tense verb 'equals' as *not* signifying the present tense or, for that matter, any tense at all. Rather, the implication of this bit of knowledge amounts to

> it is (atemporally) true that two plus two equals
> (atemporally) four.

Here we have neither an internal nor an external temporal predication and so, if at least one of the parameters must be temporal to effect the hookup with knowledge, the challenge still survives. But notice that the survival of this puzzle carries no pro-fatalist weight, for *even if* knowledge of such noncontingent propositions requires a tensed internal or external predication,[4] the battleground of the debate is focused on propositions that describe states of affairs over which we ordinarily believe we have some control. (It is no coincidence that the problem of fatalism is also known as the problem of future contingents.) Granting the temporalist victory on noncontingent propositions may affect the aesthetic simplicity of a thoroughgoing atemporal account, but the asymmetric treatment of contingent and noncontingent propositions will not persuade him one iota toward fatalism.

The fatalist's case would be strengthened by examples of contingent propositions with no internal temporal index. Such examples, conjoined with the assumption that knowledge requires either an external or an internal temporal predication of a proposition, would coerce us to accept the view that such propositions are unknowable. Perhaps statements such as 'unicorns don't exist' or 'God (where "God" is used as a "role-indicator" term) exists' are exemplars, although to many their contingency status is contentious. If the nonfatalist were to grant these examples, then, assuming he would not want to claim that we actually do not and cannot know such contingent propositions, he would need to contest the supposition that knowledge requires a temporal predication. He then faces an uncomfortable situation, for he owes an explanation of how it is possible for human beings to maintain temporal relationships, epitomized by the propositional attitudes, with atemporal entities. It should be admitted that at least on some common accounts of knowledge the temporalist does not face the same problem. For example, if we adopt a causal view of knowledge, it is much easier to understand—though by no means utterly transparent, given the difficulty of the notion of causation—how the truth of a proposition is involved in the causation of one's knowledge of the proposition if both the truth and the knowledge are temporal. The relationship seems mysterious if the cause is atemporal.

The complexity grows exponentially. A full-bodied discussion calls for a defense and an analysis of abstract and universal objects and an account of the mind that enables us to be affected by such 'third world' entities. Obviously this takes us too far afield. It might be useful, in its stead, to submit a few options that the antifatalist has at this point: (a) Challenge the temporalist to produce clear examples of contingent statements that have no explicit or implicit internal temporal parameter. (b) Admit that the explanation the temporalist desires is difficult to provide, especially adhering to a causal view of knowledge, but that nonetheless *that* we have such relationships is unquestionable; the difficulty in explanation should not subvert our certainty about the existence of what we are trying to explain. And (c) grasp the bull by the horns and submit an epistemology and a theory of mind that account for our knowledge, beliefs, hopes, and wishes about atemporal beings.

Perhaps the most poignant impetus for the tensed view of truth and facts comes from ontological considerations concerning change. It is a natural, prephilosophical belief that change is an objective feature of an external world. Not that this belief has been unchallenged; Parmenides and his disciples have denied the objectivity of change, and idealists have denied its external location. Nonetheless, most antifatalists as well as fatalists would accept the ordinary belief that change, at least of the typical sort, requires time. For an object to change is for it to don and doff properties at different times. To have a paradigmatic example at hand, consider a leaf that was green at t_1 and at a later time, t_2, was brown. We say the leaf changed color, from green to brown. Why should such mundane facts suggest that truth is a tensed notion? A temporalist might find expression for these facts in

(TC) It was true at t_1 that the leaf was green and it was true at t_2 that the leaf was brown (and false at t_1 that the leaf was brown and false at t_2 that the leaf was green).

The temporalist claims that TC expresses or reflects change. That it does so is, of course, not a matter merely of "logical form," for if the second conjunct read 'true at t_2 that the leaf weighed one ounce', no change in the leaf is entailed. It is only because green and brown are colors, and thus jointly incompatible properties of an object at a time, that TC is taken to describe genuine change.

Moreover, we notice again that an implicit use of RT* is necessary for viewing the change of color from green to brown. That is, we need to accept:

and

(a) 'The leaf was green' was true at t_1, if at t_1, the leaf was green

(b) 'The leaf was brown' was true at t_2 if at t_2 the leaf was brown.

If we didn't accept RT*, there is no reason to preclude the following:

and

(a) 'The leaf was green' was true at t_1 if at t_k, the leaf was green

(b) 'The leaf was brown' was true at t_2 if at t_j the leaf was brown,

where $t_j < t_k < t_1 < t_2$. In this scenario, the color change is just the reverse of what is intended, that is, from brown to green.

The essential point to be elicited from this is that for even a tensed notion of truth to reflect change, we need to concern ourselves with the *internal* temporal predication of propositions. External temporal predication, even if legitimate, is not sufficient for expressing change.

To further illuminate this point, consider this abortive attempt to have external temporal predication carry the burden of reflecting change.

and

(c) 'The leaf is green' was true at t_1

(d) 'The leaf is green' was false at t_2.

Change is putatively reflected in the change of truth-value of a proposition from t_1 to t_2. But if, as this argument supposes, the same proposition is undergoing a truth-value change (a change that occurs in time), it contradicts the omnitemporal view of truth to which the fatalist adheres—that the truth-value possessed by a proposition at any time is maintained by that proposition at all times.

These considerations strongly suggest the legitimacy of an atemporalist description of the color change:

(TC*)   It is (tenselessly) true that at t_1 the leaf is green and at t_2 the leaf is brown.

Many philosophers have argued that there is a special sort of change, endemic to time itself, that provides conclusive reasons for accepting tensed modalities. They have held that 'absolute becoming' ('pure becoming', 'temporal passage', 'temporal becoming', 'temporal flux') is an objective and essential component of time. On this dynamic model of time, it is a literal truth that events continually and continuously move, that they begin their lives as future, partake of the present, and journey into the ever more remote past. This view of time is opposed to a "frozen" or Minkowskian conception, where the movement of time is at best a subjective component of our experience.[5] What putatively follows from these metaphysical assumptions is a view about truth. We are now told that to accurately reflect this real feature of our world, we need a tensed as opposed to a static conception of truth. The static conception, the never-changing truths that are allegedly suggested by the atemporalist, cannot do justice to our fundamental belief that "time is a river." The division is quite neat—temporal passage is aligned with temporal truth while the frozen universe, the view that events just *are,* is befriended by atemporalism.

It is one of the great ironies in the contemporary philosophy of time that these considerations have provided for many the best reason for disavowing fatalism. In fact, they should have the opposite effect. Leaving to the side the question of which model of time is correct, the static conception of time is mirrored not in the atemporal view of truth but rather in the tensed but *omnitemporal* perspective, to which the fatalist subscribes. As has been noted, fatalism's omnitemporalism precludes change of truth-values as surely as does atemporalism (albeit for different reasons). And so if we need a theory of truth that requires change of a proposition's truth-value to reflect an objective ontological temporal dynamism, tensed truth, as conceived by fatalists, simply will not do.

Furthermore, it is difficult to understand why a truly tenseless view of truth, an atemporal view now not to be confused with omnitemporalism, should be the semantic reflection of a becomingless world. If correctly understood, an atemporal conception is completely neutral on whether there is temporal flux; the two issues are incommensurate. To think otherwise would be akin to espousing a theory that proposes that squares reflect better than triangles the fact that grass is green. Thus there is no impediment to giving a tenseless paraphrase of

    (e) 'Event E_i is future' is true at t_1 and 'E_i is present' is true at t_2 and 'E_i is past' is true at t_3

as

    (e*) It is (tenselessly) true that at t_1, E_i is future, at t_2, E_i is present, and at t_3, E_i is past.[6]

We have reached an impasse, for there seem to be no compelling arguments for either the tensed or the tenseless camp. I believe this result is quite appropriate in that the issue of tensed truth is largely a matter of decision, not discovery. Evidence for this is supplied by two different though related lines of thought.

We rely, first, on the currently popular idea of regarding propositions as functions whose inputs are possible worlds and whose outputs are truth-values (i.e., $P[W] = T/F$). We can modify this idea in two equivalent ways. We can either temporally index the possible worlds or temporally index the propositions. If we index the possible worlds, then we are using worlds at a time, temporal slices of worlds, as arguments for our propositional functions. To exemplify, let W* be our actual world, at 1/1/86. Let P be the proposition that Reagan is president. We get, then, $P(W^*) = T$; that is, the proposition that Reagan is president evaluated in α at 1/1/86 results in a truth. If we tense propositions, we have P* = Reagan is president at 1/1/86 and W = α. We get $P^*(W) = T$; that is, the proposition that Reagan is president at 1/1/86 evaluated at α results in a truth. It appears as if we have a simple way of alternating between tensed and tenseless truths. We simply use the equivalence

$$P(W^*) = T \text{ if and only if } P^*(W) = T.$$

As a second attempt, let the atemporalist grant to his adversary that propositions are tensed, that propositions are not merely true/false, but true/false at times. The atemporalist, then, stipulatively defines

> Proposition P is true at t if sh-proposition 'P at t' is sh-true.

The sh-truth of a sh-proposition obtains whenever a tenselessly true proposition obtains. Thus the original concession to the temporalist was really no more than a verbal courtesy, permission to use the terms 'proposition' and 'truth' as he liked. The moral here mirrors the moral of the first scenario: we can always find entities, call them what you like, some of which can play the role of tensed truth bearers and some of which can play the part of tenseless truth bearers.

If the question of tensed truth-bearers is a verbal one, it might seem to render the issue of fatalism substanceless. It appears that we can always avoid the fatalistic conclusion by speaking in an "atemporal mode," which at least is no worse than using a tensed language. And at worst, even if we concede the terminological jargon of 'proposition' and 'truth' to be tensed, and thus under the fatalist's jurisdiction, we can simply rewrite premises (i) and (ii) tenselessly. Thus we would have the principle of sh-bivalence, the law of the sh-excluded middle, and the sh-RT truth schema.

But perhaps the antifatalist can do more. It would be quite enlightening if we could grant the supposition of tensed truth bearers to the fatalist as a substantive victory and yet show that (iv) still rests on a questionable assumption. This is exactly what I take up now.

2.5 It is a jointly held assumption that we lack the power to change the past. That we cannot now undo or modify in any way what is already over and done with is a supposition common to fatalists and antifatalists of either stripe. We cannot now, for example, or any future time relative to 1732, make it the case that George Washington was not born at the time he was. Nor can we change the less dramatic events that occurred at that time, such as those present on this historic occasion, what their moods were at the time, or what attire the onlookers wore. This commonsense position is what grounds the plausibility of (iv), for if it was a fact from time immemorial that the 1995 sea battle will occur, preventing the sea battle would necessitate a change of the past, namely the past fact that there will be a 1995 sea battle.

There are different strategies one might employ to rebut this fatalistic gambit. One might argue that, superficial appearances to the contrary, the fact in question—that is, the fact that in 1000 b.c. there will be a sea battle in a.d. 1995—is not a fact about the past, or at least that it is not wholly a fact about the past. Rather, it is a fact (at least partly) about the year 1995, and so is a fact concerning the future. When viewed from this perspective, our ordinary belief that we can do something to prevent this future sea battle, say by having a fruitful discussion with the sea captain, does not conflict with our equally ingrained belief that the past cannot be modified. Although I believe this is a fruitful avenue to pursue, I wish to take a quite different route. For my purposes, I will grant that this fact is a fact wholly about the year 1000 b.c., in the sense that its constitution, its fulfillment, is complete and over and done with by 1000 b.c. It is, then, to use Ockhamistic jargon, to be granted that this is a hard fact.[7] The question then is to reconcile this concession with the falsity of (iv). We need first to see that this commonsense position concerning the past's fixity, soon to be formulated somewhat more rigorously, should not be viewed as conflicting with the more controversial doctrine of retrocausation. Retrocausation, or backward causation, is the view that it is at least logically possible for some causes to postdate some effects. The thesis of the unchangeability of the past does not preclude that some events might be caused by subsequent events, but only that once the constitution is complete, whether effected by ordinary forward causation, backward causation, random happenings, or whatever, it cannot be altered at some later time.

Next, let us supply the conditions under which, per impossibile, a person could change the past, conditions we can assume are amenable to both fatalist and antifatalist.

(CP)   P can change the past if P can perform some action A
         such that either A itself would be a past-changing event
         or A would cause a past-changing event.[8]

However, the antifatalist may claim that although no one can change
the past—as now understood in CP—one should not infer that

(CP*)   P cannot perform some action A* such that if A* were
         performed, the past, relative to A*'s occurrence, would
         have been differently constituted than had A* not been
         performed.

The antifatalist then holds that we have the power to prevent the
upcoming sea battle, perhaps by speaking with the captain. The exercise
of this power would not cause any modification of the past. Rather, (i) it
would cause the past to have a certain constitution that it would have
lacked had the power not been exercised (here, retrocausation is assumed), or (ii) the constitution would have been a causal consequent of a
past other than the one that would have obtained had the power been
unexercised (here, forward causation is assumed), or (iii) the constitution of the past would have been acausally different from the one that
would have obtained had the power not been exercised (here lack of
causation is assumed).[9]

2.6 We are now in a position to take stock. Fatalism becomes a
plausible thesis, that is, RF and RF' become persuasive arguments,
under, minimally, the following presuppositions: (a) it is a substantive
truth that facts and truths are tensed; (b) modified tensed versions of
LEM and RT, that is, LEM* and RT*, are acceptable; and (c) CP* is
affirmed. Undoubtedly, individuals will differ in their opinions of the
absolute and relative plausibility of (a), (b), and (c). If this is subjectivism, then it is a subjectivism with which we can and—indeed in
philosophy, at least—must live.

THREE

FATALISM, DETERMINISM, AND FREEDOM

TOWARD THE PAST

3.1 "Determinism," like "fatalism," is in large measure a term of art. Thus the borders surrounding permissible analyses or definitions are rather vague. The main concern, for our purposes, in giving any rigorous formulation of the notion is that it contain some implication of some sort of necessity, for it is only if this concept is integral to the thesis of determinism that the traditional discussions of determinism and freedom will prove intelligible. After all, *the* free will problem, if any question in this area deserves the appellation, is whether determinism is compatible with personal freedom. To give an account of determinism without an essential mention of necessity is to make a farce of the history of the problem. Indeed, such a characterization of determinism would do a disservice to compatibilists as well as incompatibilists. If there were no prima facie plausibility to the idea that determinism and freedom conflict, one would hardly need to *defend* either position; the debate would disintegrate before it began. This is not to suggest that these two doctrines will not, after review, be demonstrated as jointly consistent; rather, on pain of viewing all past participants in the debate as hopelessly misguided if not just plain stupid, we need to give some account of determinism where adherence to incompatibilism is understandable.

A perhaps propitious way to begin is to think of determinism as the thesis that claims, as fatalism does, that whatever occurs must (necessarily) occur. This formulation serves the heuristic function of reminding us that, superficially at least, determinism and fatalism (in either logical or metaphysical guise) share significant traits. They both, for example, espouse a thesis concerning the necessity of events or states of affairs. It also points out the way we can focus on their differences, for if these two theses are not to be identical, the 'must' of determinism will differ from both the logical 'must' of logical fatalism and the metaphysical 'must' of metaphysical fatalism. Our task, then, is to characterize deterministic necessity.

The intuitive, unrefined idea is forwarded by the following reflections. The world works in certain ways that continually exhibit regularities. Books fall when dropped, bread nourishes when eaten, windows shatter when greeted by fast-moving massive objects, and so on. Let us call these ways the world works 'laws of nature'. Thus, for example, it is a law of nature that unimpeded objects, when dropped from a distance near the surface of the earth, will fall toward the earth's center. The term 'law' is used suggestively—violations of natural laws are naturally impossible. Voluntaristically put, one cannot perform any action such that the performance of that action would result in the violation of a law of nature, where the 'cannot' is taken naturally or empirically. In this sense laws of nature, ways of the world's workings, govern or dictate which events are to form the natural constitution of the actual world.

It is not unreasonable to suppose that, given the existence of some events, which themselves have been dictated by these natural laws, and the governing laws themselves, a unique result eventuates, in the form of other events. One might think of the laws of nature as functions that operate upon events, resulting in a particular output consisting of other events. Once the function and the input are settled, the output is necessitated; 'necessitated' now, in the very strong logical or conceptual sense. To implement a mathematical analogy, let $f(x) = 5X + 2$, and let the input to this function be 3. The output of $f(3)$, which is 17, is a mathematically coerced result relative to the function and input. Just as any other result, given this function and input, is a mathematical or logical impossibility—a violation of the laws of mathematics or logic—

any event other than the one that actually occurs in the natural world, given the actual events (input) and the laws of nature (function), is also a logical impossibility. Moreover—and this is an additional benefit about using the mathematical analogy—determinism has no essential temporal parameters. If determinism is true, then every event, regardless of its date or tense relative to any other set of events, is naturally determined or necessitated. As with fatalism, determinism's scope is all-encompassing, and as with our discussion of fatalism, we may circumscribe our discussion of determinism to include only its effect over future events, since it is surely over these events that we commonsensically believe we have some power, and so it is concerning these events that conflicts regarding freedom and necessity naturally arise. It would be far more distressing to find that the truth of determinism precludes our ability to affect the constitution of the future than to discover that determinism (even if nothing otherwise would) exempts us from having the power to affect the constitution of the past.

We can now offer a definition.

Determinism = $_{df.}$ (The thesis claims that) it is logically impossible that there are any worlds with natural laws and pasts that are congruent with the actual world's and yet have futures that diverge from the actual world's.[1]

It is with this understanding of determinism that we can make sense of what the determinist means by claiming that whatever happens must happen. That is, the determinist's 'must' ('necessity') amounts to the claim that an event in the actual world is determined if it appears in every logically possible world that shares both the natural laws and the past of the actual world.

It might prove useful to put the point differently. Let t_5 be the present moment, and consider all the logically possible worlds with the laws of the actual world that are identical to our world up to this point, at least in terms of their natural pasts. This subset of all the logically possible worlds is, for our purposes, identical to the actual world. (It is worth noting that these logically possible worlds are not all identical simpliciter. For one thing, it surely seems logically possible that there are nonnatural events and that some but not all of the worlds naturally identical to the actual world possess some of these events.) Determinism entails that these worlds all (naturally) identical up to and including t_5 will remain identical forever; in this select subset of logically possible worlds, there will be no distinct futures.

Let me clarify why a unique future depends on maintaining the actual world's natural laws as well as its past. Consider first a logically possible world congruent with the actual world up to and including t_5, but immediately afterward containing a new and different set of natural laws. There is obviously no inclination to believe that this world's future will be anything like, let alone identical to, that of the actual world. Indeed, this is an understatement, for if the laws are diametrically opposed—that is, inconsistent—then although both worlds up to t_5 contained the falling of dropped books and the nourishment of persons who ate bread, such regularities would discontinue in the logical world with new natural laws. Now, in this world dropped books may go up and bread eaters may starve; in short, all bets are off regarding the world's future constitution. Consider, second, logically possible worlds whose natural laws (means of operation) are unflaggingly identical to those of the actual world but whose natural past is decidedly distinct from the actual world's. In some of these worlds, though not all, the future will differ from that of the actual world, for in some such worlds, although books would fall if dropped unimpeded, there are, unlike the actual world, no books for the asking.

Thus understood, determinism is neutral regarding the modal status of both the natural laws and (past) events. That is, a determinist need not take a position on whether either the natural laws or past events are logically (or metaphysically, for that matter) necessitated. Historically, determinists have rejected the offer to consider the laws and (past) events as logically necessitated; they have rejected logical fatalism, but as I have defined determinism, there is no conceptual obstacle to forming this alliance. Conversely, it is evident that the logical fatalist is committed to determinism. This entailment is trivial once we recall that the logical fatalist holds that there are no logically possible worlds other than the actual world. We have, then, logical fatalism entailing but not being entailed by determinism.

The relation between determinism and metaphysical fatalism is not so simple. The metaphysical fatalist, unlike his counterpart, allows for distinct logically possible worlds. Since the necessity the metaphysical fatalist imputes to future events is past necessity, that is, the necessity imputed to past events relative to our present abilities, a clear understanding of his necessity requires articulation of past necessity itself. What we need to do, in other words, is give an elucidation of what the inviolability or fixity of the past amounts to and then compare it with our account of deterministic necessity. This requires a twofold strategy. I begin with trying to understand the sense in which the past is inviolable—the modal status of the necessity of the past. Part and parcel of this discussion is elucidating the relation between our current abilities and past events: In what ways, if any, is it correct to claim that we cannot alter the past? Second, we need to investigate the relation between deterministically necessitated events and our ability to perform actions. This in effect is the crucial question in the free will debate. This second task is further justified by its obvious importance independent of any ramifications it has for our understanding of fatalism.

3.2   It must be admitted that our belief in the past's unchangeability (fixity, inviolability) is one of our most basic and natural beliefs and that stating the exact nature of this belief, along with its justification, is typically viewed as superfluous. Virtually whenever this belief is articulated, it serves the purpose of an obvious and unquestioned premise from which other more interesting results can be derived. This assumption is most conspicuous in many arguments concerning the incompatibility of determinism and freedom.[2] The question before us is whether such a cavalier attitude is warranted.

The claim that the past is unchangeable amounts, for our voluntaristic purposes, to the claim that we have no ability to alter or modify the past in any way. What does *not* form part of our natural belief, and is not entailed by this natural belief, is that it is (logically or empirically) impossible to try to bring about an alteration in the past. Indeed this may be impossible; but if it is, its impossibility—logical or empirical—does not follow merely from the fact, if it is one, that we necessarily lack the ability to modify the past. Consider, as an example of trying to do what cannot be done, attempts to square the circle. We now know that the area of any circle cannot equal the area of any square (owing to the nature of π), but it appears that persons have tried to show that such identities exist. At the very least this is a natural description of what they were trying to do (the practitioners themselves would describe it as such), and it would only be in the grip of a philosophical theory that we would wish to pervert this commonsense account. Similarly, mathematicians and laymen have tried (or at least once again it certainly seems so) to discover solutions to $x^n + y^n = z^n$ ($n > 2$). It may well turn out that we find that success is logically impossible; nonetheless, characterizing these persons' actions as "attempts" hardly seems perverted.

Most philosophers take the impossibility of changing the past to be logical or conceptual. It is not merely that we lack certain physical or physiological skills with which evolution or God may later endow us so that this deficiency becomes rectified. Nor is it merely that natural laws doom such a project. Rather, it is claimed that a change in the past would present us with a logically inconsistent state of affairs. It is for this reason that the ability to change the past cannot—now taken as 'logically cannot'—exist. Even God, as we might picturesquely put it, cannot change the past.

If, then, the impossibility of our altering the past is a consequence of such an alteration's being logically inconsistent, one would expect that we could precisely situate where such an inconsistency occurs. If we assume that we have the ability to alter the past, we should involve ourselves, as with any reductio argument, in a self-contradiction.

I think that both of the following batteries of statements fairly capture what the ability to change the past amounts to—that is, what would be required if such an ability could (logically) exist.

(A) (i) At t_1, past event E_p with qualities Q_p, exists.

   (ii) J has the ability at t_2 to change E_p.

   (iii) J instantiates his ability at t_2.

   (iv) After t_2, E_p and $\sim Q_p$ exist.

(B) (i*) At t_1, E_p exists.

　(ii*) J has the ability at t_2 to change E_p.

　(iii*) J instantiates his ability at t_2.

　(iv*) After t_2, $\sim E_p$ exists.

The difference between (A) and (B) manifests the difference between Aristotle's notions of qualitative change and substantive change. Roughly, the distinction is that only in qualitative changes does the object undergoing the alteration persist. Qualitative change is the typical, garden-variety change we are all associated with. To say, for example, that a person has the ability at a particular time to change the color of a rod from blue to green is to say that he has the ability, at a certain time, to make what was a blue rod become a green rod. At one time the rod is a particular color, and at some later time, after the ability is exemplified, the same rod is a different color. The persisting object here is the rod. This is to be opposed to substantive change, where the object in question is created or obliterated. To have the ability to substantively change a past event Ep would be to have the ability to bring about, at some particular time, $\sim E_p$. This more drastic sort of change is an instantiation of our ability, at some time, to eradicate the particular rod. One can understand substantive change as encompassing qualitative change, since to effect a substantive change is to bring about a host of qualitative changes. When the rod is destroyed, then qualities such as that rod's color, shape, and texture are also destroyed; when E_p is substantively changed, none of the qualities of E_p persist. The natural belief that the past cannot be altered is applicable to both sorts of changes. We believe both that we cannot undo a past event and that we cannot alter the most minute detail of any past event. So, for example, if I lost my wallet in Dallas in 1980, not only do I now necessarily lack the ability to not lose my wallet in Dallas in 1980, but I currently cannot lose a different wallet in Dallas in 1980 or make the lost wallet a different color or texture than the one that was actually lost. If alteration of the past involves a contradiction, inconsistencies should be implicit in both (A) and (B).

Ordinarily, we think of human abilities as items we can gain and lose in time. I now, for example, have the ability to make a twenty-foot jump shot, whereas some thirty-five years ago, when I was a small child, I lacked such an ability. Furthermore, there is good reason to suppose that when I am ninety years old (if I ever reach that age), this ability will no longer be with me. These considerations justify the use of a temporal reference regarding the possession of an ability. One might argue that one can have the ability, at a certain time, to perform some action only at some later time. So, for example, perhaps I now have the ability to fly to New York tomorrow (whereas I now lack the ability to fly to New York today). On this view, the acts I am able to perform also require a temporal reference, and so a complete description of an ability requires a double temporal reference—one time denoting when the ability is possessed and another, perhaps distinct, time denoting when the act is to be performed. A person who holds this view may claim that as an infant I had the ability to sink a twenty-foot jump shot thirty-five years later, and that talk of making a twenty-foot jump shot is itself significantly incomplete, since it omits a temporal reference. If convention or context makes it clear that the two temporal references denote the same time, one explicit reference, if not both, may be omitted. Still, continues the double temporal reference apologist, the conceptual point remains that abilities require dual time references.

Fortunately, we need not become embroiled in these issues. Our belief in our inability to change the past extends omnitemporally. Thus the commonsense belief is that we at no time have the ability to change at any time the constitution of the past. Thus, even if the requirement of the double temporal reference is conceded, it can easily be accommodated by this somewhat expanded version of our natural belief.

To further help us understand in what a change or an alteration of the past consists, we should compare our natural belief in the necessary inability to do so with an ability that is not so automatically denied. Recall the Lewis gambit introduced in chapter 2. Lewis, trying to demonstrate the inconclusiveness of Peter van Inwagen's attempt to prove the incompatibility of freedom and determinism, claims that no reason has been produced to show that we lack the ability, let alone necessarily lack the ability, to perform an action such that if the action were performed the past would be differently constituted than had we not performed that action. Here, as Lewis himself is at pains to point out, there is no hint that we possess the ability to alter the past. Moreover, since he claims this is a way of avoiding incompatibilism, this ability portrayed in the Lewis gambit needs to be consistent with determinism. If the agent performs action A, which he is free to perform, rather than action B, which he is also free to perform, the past that determines his performance of A would be differently constituted than it would have been had the agent freely chosen to perform B. Of course, had he performed B, this differently constituted past, under the aegis of determinism, would have determined his performance of B.

It would be misleading to even characterize the implementation of this Lewis ability as a way of *affecting* the past, for 'affecting', like 'modifying', 'changing', and 'altering', is a verb that suggests, if not entails, causal efficacy. Of course one could delete this implication from the term 'affect' and just defend it in such a way that is compatible with the instantiation of the Lewis ability. In this trivial sense, then, Lewis could be seen as suggesting that, although the past cannot be changed, it can be affected. Obviously nothing philosophically substantive would have happened in such verbal maneuvering. Indeed, it is best to view the Lewis ability as sidestepping the whole notion of bringing something about, whether causally or acausally. It is more profitable to view the exemplification of the ability as a sufficient condition of the past's being constituted in a particular way. Just as the knowledge of a proposition is sufficient for its truth and yet does not in general bring about or cause the proposition's truth, so is the implemented Lewis ability sufficient for the past's being constituted in a particular way.

To clarify, imagine the Lewis gambit being applied to the future. The ability, then, would be the ability to perform some actions such that if they were performed the future would be constituted differently than had the ability not been implemented. This is hardly a shocking thesis, for it is merely a version of our commonsense belief that the future's constitution, unlike the past's, can be influenced by our current actions. Aphoristically, we naturally believe that, although the past is closed, the future is open. Here there is no temptation to take the implemented

Lewis ability as constituting a *change* of the future; rather, the implemented ability is necessary for the future to contain the events it does.

Note that although Lewis's strategy is not formally inconsistent with the inalterability of the past, it is to say the least contentious. Consider Jane, who received a C in last semester's philosophy course. Being a Lewisian and a determinist, she assumes that she is now able (free) to study for her current philosophy class. Her belief in determinism has her believe that, necessarily, the constitution of the past (along with nature's laws) makes it the case that she will study or makes it the case that she will not. She decides to study and does so, hoping that this is an action sufficient for the past's being constituted differently than it actually is, specifically hoping that this past include Jane's receiving an A and not a C in last semester's philosophy class. She realizes that her studying cannot alter her past grade (she has the natural belief in the fixity of the past), but she hopes that the implementation of this ability that Lewis tells us we have is indicative of (is a necessary condition of) an alternatively constituted past. After studying, she looks at last semester's grades and notices a C in Philosophy 101.

We can assume that a similar scenario would occur repeatedly. Of course it is a gross simplification to think that of all the indefinitely many actions Jane could perform, the choice to pick the relevant act that constitutes the sufficient condition for a counterfactually comprised past would conflate to a choice between performing or not performing a particular action. Nonetheless, if this is the Lewisian response, it does seem rather lame, for it makes it appear that the lack of a sufficient condition for the alternatively constituted past is just a matter of luck or coincidence and not, as at least it intuitively appears, in the "nature of things." Still, with all this being said, the Lewis gambit, if ultimately unsatisfying, is not lacking owing to any fault in logic, and this may well satisfy those who, like Lewis, just desire a formal way of escaping the entailment from determinism to the lack of freedom or the eradication of abilities.

Let us now return to (A) and its putative self-inconsistency. It is evident that there are no two statements that are overtly in the form of 'p and ~ p', and so if logical impossibility or self-contradiction is to be shown some further manipulations on claims (i–iv), or (i*–iv*), will be needed.

Perhaps having a concrete example at hand will be useful. Imagine someone claims to have the ability in 1988 to alter the start of World War I. He admits, indeed insists, that before the implementation of this ability that he is now about to undertake, World War I began in 1914, but that after his ability is instantiated World War I will no longer have begun in 1914 (we need not worry in which, if any, year World War I is now supposed to have begun). He attests then to the joint truth of

and

(a)   Before 1988, World War I began in 1914

(b)   As of 1988, World War I did not begin in 1914.

I should emphasize that implementation of this ability is not to be understood in some weakened epistemic sense. The claim is not that he has an ability to discover the true origin of World War I—to discover, that is, that its real beginning was not, as previously believed, in 1914. The ability is to be understood in a stronger ontological sense—the ability to change the starting date of the First World War. It is to be viewed precisely in the way we understand a person's ability to change the color of a rod from blue to green.

We would consider (a) and (b) as contradictories if the temporal introductions ('before 1988', 'as of 1988') were vacuous, that is, if (a) reduced to (meant no more than) 'World War I began in 1914' and (b) reduced to 'World War I did not begin in 1914'. And perhaps one way of beginning to argue for this position is to argue for the senselessness of tensing dates or temporalizing truths. We have already had a somewhat extended discussion of this issue (cf. chap. 2), but one addition can be made. If this is the strategy to be employed in arguing for the un-changeability of the past, the entire debate between the modifiability or unmodifiability of the past disintegrates. Although we are disallowed ways of expressing alterability, we are by the same token precluded by language from expressing inalterability. We must keep in mind that omnitemporal language ('always', 'never') is still temporal language, and so if expressions such as 'before 1988' are verboten, thus making changeability an inexpressible concept, parity of reasoning makes expressions such as 'always' unusable, thus evacuating meaning from the notion of unchangeability. It would no longer make any sense to speak of the inalterability (fixity) of the past, which is held to be the common-sense notion. The general principle employed here is that if one term is considered senseless or in some way illegitimate, then the negation of this term must also be considered senseless or illegitimate. If it makes no sense to speak of the alterability of the past, then it makes no sense to speak of the past's inalterability.

If alteration of the past committed one to the view that an event both occurred and did not occur at a particular time simpliciter, then changing the past would involve a contradiction, and so any claim to having an ability to so alter the past would necessarily be false. But as (A) and (B) make clear, such a commitment is not entailed by adhering to the possibility of changing the past. The past is differently constituted *at different times* if one successfully implements one's ability, and this, at least so far, has not been shown to be incoherent.

Perhaps conceptual incoherence can be shown in quite a different way. Using this tack, an incoherence can be shown by investigating language, specifically the language of intentions, aims, goals, and so forth. All these terms, and the attitudes they reflect, are future oriented. Taken as a logical or conceptual claim, this amounts to claiming that the very meaning of 'intention', 'aim', and such mandates the future-directed orientation of the corresponding attitudes. But this seems to trivialize our belief in the unchangeability of the past, for it makes this unchangeability reside in facts about how we use language. If this were all there was to the matter, we might invent the concepts of sh-intentions, sh-goals, and sh-plans, which are to be understood as just like their more common counterparts, but without the alleged conceptual implications they have with the constitutions of the past and future. A precluded question concerning intentions is now transformed into a permissible one regarding sh-intentions: Why can we only sh-intend to perform actions that will have efficacy toward the future? The chore for the apologist of the conceptual impossibility of changing the past becomes demonstrating why sh-intending a past event is logically inconsistent.

Perhaps it would prove useful to compare our belief in the inviolability of the past with our equally ingrained belief in the openness of the future, the view that we currently have the ability to affect the future's constitution. Assuming, provisionally at least, that the two beliefs form mirror images of each other, we can cast our future-oriented belief in the following battery of statements

(C) (i**)   At t_2, future event F_p with qualities Z_p exists.

    (ii**)   J has the ability at t_1 to change F_p.

    (iii**) J instantiates his ability at t_1.

    (iv**) After t_1, F_p and $\sim Z_p$ exist.

Since (C), ex hypothesi, represents our allegedly consistent view of the relation between our current abilities and a future event, there had better not be a contradiction to be found among (i**–iv**). Thus *if* one can demonstrate an inconsistency in (A), one must be prepared to defend the charge that such an inconsistency can be transported to (C). This helps make clear why a certain frequently voiced attempt to manifest an inconsistency in (A) is doomed. One often hears that if an event exists—already exists—then there is nothing one can do to alter it. But in any way that this is not taken as question-begging, its truth would coerce us into accepting (C) as manifesting an inconsistency. The 'exists' that appears in both (i) and (i**) should be understood as temporally neutral. We could, if we wished, have rewritten (i) and (i**) as

    (iW)   Relative to t_2, E_p with Q_p existed

and

    (i**W)   Relative to t_1, P_p with Z_p will exist,

where the notion of existence is now tensed; tensed in the past in (iW) and in the future in (i**W). But how can this help show a relevant disanalogy between (A) and (C)? The only difference, once again, is that of tense, but this cannot serve us since the very question at issue is to discover why the past, unlike the future, is not susceptible to our present abilities.

Some philosophers have thought that the resolution is obvious once

73

we make a distinction between changing a tense and affecting the constitution of a tense. They have claimed that we cannot change either the past or the future, but that the past and the past alone is unable to be influenced by any of our actions. However, this offers us no aid. First and foremost, we are questioning why the past differs from the future relative to our current abilities, and drawing this distinction adds nothing to the mere assertion that the future, unlike the past, can be influenced. Second, why accept the unchangeability of the future? Most would consider it a sophomoric modal fallacy to argue *simply* from the fact that an event will occur that it cannot be changed. At most what will be conceded is that such an event will not be altered.[3] Here an analogy with the concept of knowledge is instructive. From the truth of 'S knows that p', merely the truth of p and not its necessity can be inferred. What holds for facts that we know holds for events that will occur.

Perhaps lurking behind this is an allegedly somewhat more sophisticated idea. The future, unlike the past, is said to be empty; that is, the future does not exist until the time when it is brought about. It is brought about, in large measure, by the implementation of our current abilities, at which time the future becomes present and soon thereafter past. On this view, (ii**) would be necessarily false since, necessarily, there can be no F_p. The past, on the other hand, is full; it exists the moment after it is brought about.

There is, I think, a mass of confusion that makes up this view, but even if we grant its cogency, it goes no way in helping us understand why the constitution of the past is not susceptible to our present abilities. We still need to know why fullness forbids, whereas emptiness permits, the implementation of our abilities to matter. Whatever use these metaphors have, they do nothing to make us believe in the logical inconsistency of past-oriented abilities.

Somewhat along the same lines, one can imagine trying to take advantage of the notion of determinateness. An event is determinate if and only if for every property P, that event either has or lacks P. Suppose it is granted that past events are determinate, whereas future events are not (perhaps determinateness is definitive of pastness). How is this to help us see that the future alone is amenable to our present abilities? The suggestion is that the past's determinateness (or definiteness) leaves us no room to operate, whereas the future's indeterminateness (or indefiniteness) gives us some maneuverability. (This, I gather, is virtually, if not veritably, the picture of the empty versus full tenses.)

But the question why the determinate cannot be altered persists. It is not obvious, that is, why merely because of the determinateness of an event, such an event cannot be modified. To see this, consider what our attitude would be toward a past event that was indeterminate. If this (logical) possibility is allowed, it seems that the intuition concerning the fixity of the past still holds. Similarly, consider once again if it is granted that there is such a possibility, that a future event is determinate. I take it that our belief concerning the openness of this future event would still hold. This suggests that it is the pastness or futurity of an event rather than the status of its determinateness that alone accounts for the nature of our beliefs regarding the event's susceptibility to our current actions. If determinateness plays any role whatever, it cannot be an *explanatory* one. We still, then, have not been able to justify our beliefs regarding the inviolability of the past.

3.3 We have heretofore operated under the supposition that the reasons for our belief concerning the closedness of the past are a priori; that is, that the reasons we believe in the impotence of our current actions to modify the past are independent of our experience and can be reduced to logical considerations. Perhaps this assumption is incorrect, and the true basis for our belief resides in our ordinary experience. On this view it is sensible to speak of having desires, intentions, plans, and so forth to modify the past. There is no logical impediment to the satisfaction of these mental psychologies. Rather, that we cannot alter the past is known a posteriori.

One may argue that this impotence toward the past, now viewed as an empirical generalization, is based on numerous failed attempts to try to modify the past. Just as our claim that a baseball player cannot hit a ball nine hundred feet is based on the failure of such attempts, so too is our inability to alter the past founded on unsuccessful tries to make the past different. Just as laws of physics and physiology preclude a human's hitting a baseball that far, the laws of physics and psychology make it impossible for one to fulfill an intention or a plan to modify the past.

One problem with this a posteriori justification is that, as a matter of fact, persons do not intend or try to alter the past. But this fact needs explanation. It simply will not do, as an attempt to resurrect the logical character of the past's fixity, to claim that logical impossibility precludes such attempts. After all, there have been countless attempts to square the circle or to trisect an angle with only a compass and straightedge. Nor will it do to explain the lack of attempts on the fact that persons know the logical impossibility of such an endeavor (unlike the cases where persons have tried to square circles or trisect angles). Even under the dubious assumption that the person on the street acknowledges a distinction between logical and empirical impossibility, we have tried, unsuccessfully, to discover exactly where such an alleged logical inconsistency is situated.

But perhaps the assertion that past-altering attempts are not made is simply not true. Indeed, there are cases where "primitive peoples" and religious persons have acted in a manner that might be described in this way. Usually such cases are described as attempts by unsophisticated persons to try to bring about a past, simpliciter, other than the actual one.[4] These tries have been ridiculed by pointing out that it is a logical contradiction for an event to both occur and not occur at a particular time. But as we have seen, a more charitable and more complex idea may be lurking behind such endeavors. We might understand such attempts as attempts to change the past *relative* to certain times. So, for example, if a mother prays to a supernatural being for her son's death of five years earlier not to have happened, we might understand this wish not as a plea to God to make her dead son alive, simpliciter, but to make it the case *now,* five years hence, that her son no longer be dead. Most mothers, I take it, would be quite satisfied that, although as of yesterday her son was dead five years ago, relative to today her son is alive. And as we have seen, if there is something logically incoherent about this, it is not strikingly obvious. The a posteriori justification then takes the assumed lack of success, perhaps universal lack of success, as indicating that the laws of nature make it impossible for any past-altering enterprise to work.

Such a justification may well involve physical laws concerning entropy, possibly along with the second law of thermodynamics. Perhaps such physical considerations would entail the impossibility of altering the past. Unlike the prior reasoning, such an attempt would not directly involve examining failed intentions but would explain why it is that such intentions are doomed to fail. The general idea would be that increases of entropy are inevitable given the way our world happens to be, and any alteration of the past would violate such natural dictates. The niceties of the physics involved are not necessary for the major point: just as, say, we are assured that a baseball layer will not hit a ball farther than nine hundred feet from knowledge concerning physics and physiology (as opposed, now, to viewing countless failed attempts), we are similarly assured of the failure of attempts to alter the past from considerations of entropy (homogeneity) and thermodynamics (as opposed, now, to viewing the [relatively] few failed attempts to do so).

This last account is plausible; but even if this is ultimately an incorrect account of the nature of the necessity of past events, I have tried to give reasons for thinking that an experience-based rather than a logic-based explanation holds out the greatest hope. Insofar as natural laws would be broken if the past were altered (and not, as many believe, laws of logic), the inviolability of the past extends only so far as one accepts the "inviolability" of the relevant natural laws. What this fixity amounts to is a large issue that I will not deal with. Instead, I will now turn to the relation between the necessity of a determined event and our free will concerning such necessity. To make progress here, some backtracking will be necessary. Some conclusions already reached will be iterated, but their mode of production will differ in, I hope, a salutary manner.

3.4 Perhaps the central issue in the cluster of issues that constitute "the free will problem" is whether the free will of individuals is (logically) consistent with the existence of a deterministic world. (Let us call this the compatibility problem.) I want to step back from the intricacies of the debate as much as possible in an attempt to investigate the general landscape of the battlefield. In doing so, I shall suggest that perhaps the antagonism between those who believe in the consistency of

77

free will and determinism (compatibilists) and those who do not (in-compatibilists) is ill deserved. The plausibility of this rather deflationary result will depend on how powerful a case can be made that these two parties lack enough common ground to make a conflict possible.

What may initially strike one as bizarre is that the compatibility problem should prove so difficult. Why should a decision regarding the consistency or inconsistency of

(i)   determinism is true

(ii)   individuals have free will

prove intractable? Typically, the joint logical (in)consistency of statements is not a hotly debated topic. Few, for example, would contest the joint inconsistency of

(a)   there is life on other planets

(b)   there is not life on other planets

or the consistency of

(c)   there is life on other planets

(d)   there are no chickens on other planets.

It seems that all that is necessary to resolve such issues, of which (a–d) are admittedly simplified examples, is to get clear about the meanings of the terms involved. After this is accomplished, there is nothing much else to do than *see* whether the conjunction of the relevant pair (or triad, etc.) of statements forms a contradiction.

Yet, apparently, philosophy is never so simple. Consider, for example, the time-honored problem of evil. In this theological case, we try to ascertain whether

(iii)   God exists

is consistent with

(iv)   evil exists,

78

that is, whether God (logically) can exist in an evil-infested world. Surely there can be disagreements about the meanings of 'God' and 'evil' (or, what will not add a new dimension for our purposes, the respective natures of God and evil),[5] but if concurrence can be reached on these matters, the issue of consistency should evaporate. In broadest perspective, how can questions of (logical) consistency be anything more than verbal quibbles? This is not to denigrate the problem of evil. Discussions concerning the nature of God and evil are significant in many persons' lives, and not in the purely intellectual way that the compatibility problem manifests, and perhaps must manifest, itself. Nonetheless, it is one thing to claim that a philosophical puzzle is a verbal issue and quite another to show that it is.

Obviously, to have any hope of resolving the compatibility issue, we need a firm grasp on the two key terms 'determinism' and 'free will'. But even before we seek such accounts (definitions, analyses), it is important to note what parameters need to surround them. At first blush this call for limits may appear unduly restrictive, for surely philosophers can define terms any way they wish. The only requirement, if one wants to call it that, is that the proffered analyses be clear.

This attitude of tolerance is a bit misleading. If the participants in this debate analyze the key terms so that they have little or no resemblance to the ways these terms are ordinarily used (assuming for the moment that there are such ordinary ways), there is no logical impediment to their doing so. Yet though constraints on the analyses of the two key terms 'determinism' and 'free will' are not logically mandated, they are effected by the supposition that the compatibility problem is a substantive, nontechnical problem—one that naturally suggests itself to many reflective persons. John Bramhall, whose debate with Hobbes in the mid-seventeenth century signaled the beginning of the modern period's fascination with the free will problem, was bishop of Derry, and undoubtedly many in their audience would hardly consider themselves philosophers. And if I may be allowed an autobiographical note, my own interest in the issue began when I was a young teenager, at a stage in my "philosophical" career when I would not have known a Berkeleyan tree if it had hit me in the head.

The point is not that philosophers cannot, by the use of technical or stipulative accounts, formulate a puzzle and label it the "compatibility problem." The point is that such a transformation loses touch with the problem we are really concerned with. If this does happen, however, if a technical problem replaces the apparently baffling question that served as its origin, we might very well adopt an attitude of indifference. We, as reflective men and women who think about the status of what seems to be our freedom in what seems to be a deterministic world (at least at first), need not be sidetracked into a debate whose content has merely a nominal resemblance to the problem we found legitimately puzzling.

Returning to the perennial paradox of the problem of evil, it would hardly be satisfying to be told that the joint consistency of (iii) and (iv) has been demonstrated by defining 'God' as 'a being with a great but limited powers'. This is unsatisfying because it is evasive. The problem—the very real problem that intrudes on the minds of many reflective persons—rests on the ordinary concept of the Judeo-Christian God. This concept sees God as an omniscient, omnibenevolent, omnipotent entity, and any solution to the problem of evil needs to take this as its starting point. Naturally, exactly what these attributes of God amount to is a matter needing elucidation, but to be significant, it must be an elucidation of our ordinary concept of the Deity.

Far from denigrating the noble ambition of articulating, clarifying, disambiguating, and making precise nontechnical language, these comments should be construed as an apology for these pursuits. Indeed, when imprecision, ambiguity, and lack of clarity are removed, what seemed problematic may cease to appear so. In effect, this was Hume's contention concerning the free will controversy—that once the disputants had a clear view of the relevant terminology, once they fully understood what 'necessity' ('determination') and 'liberty' ('freedom') meant—the entire debate would dissolve into unanimous agreement on behalf of compatibilism. The evaluation of Hume's dialectic to the side, we need to remind ourselves that to clarify and articulate is not to stipulate or create.

Since so much of importance depends on the distinction between analyzing (clarifying, articulating, elucidating) an ordinary, nontechnical concept and creating (inventing, suggesting, stipulating, inaugurating) a nonordinary, technical one, one would think that philosophers would take great pains to disseminate to their audience which task they take themselves to be engaging in. This, unfortunately, has not in general been the case. Furthermore, some philosophers, and I will exemplify this presently, seem to misrepresent themselves; that is, they take themselves to be engaging in elucidation, whereas the task they are actually undertaking is a creative one. The results, as one would suspect, are disastrous; discussions pass each other by, with any points of contact being random and peripheral.

The obvious question to be broached, then, is how we are to determine whether we are giving "analyses" of ordinary concepts or creating concepts that are technical and extraordinary. The final arbiter can only be how well the account of the concept matches the way the concept is ordinarily used. If we wish to know whether a given account is of an ordinary concept, we need to see whether typical users of the language take this account as descriptive of their general linguistic practices. Dictionaries, by and large, record how typical language users employ terms. In effect, dictionaries codify accounts of ordinary concepts. Lexicographers, after all, are empirical scientists who conduct sociological inquiries using language use as their data in order to discover the meanings of terms. This is virtually (but not quite totally) what "conceptual analysis" seems to amount to. In short, then, and somewhat roughly, the criterion for successful elucidation of an ordinary concept is that, generally, language users accept the articulation as a more or less accurate description of what they mean by the concept. A look at part of the Berkeleyan enterprise will help bring this discussion into focus.

3.5   Berkeley, most assuredly, saw himself as a philosopher of common sense. Part of this self-perspective included being a descriptivist concerning our conceptual scheme. That is, he saw his metaphysical and linguistic philosophies as elucidating our commonsense ontological scheme and our ordinary linguistic practices. We will investigate whether Berkeley's

self-view was accurate, but let me point out that this view is not platitudinous, that there have been philosophers who proudly aver that they
are engaged in revisionism. Spinoza is one who announces that he is
adopting a technical vocabulary, believing that our ordinary lexicon is
too imprecise an instrument with which to conduct his inquiries. Like
his vocabulary, Spinoza's ontology is hardly ordinary; we need go no
further than recognizing that Spinoza's God is in many ways essentially
different from his Judeo-Christian counterpart.

The defense of Berkeleyan descriptivism would begin by noting that
Berkeley's use of the term 'book', for example, virtually coincides with
that of the typical speaker. Berkeley would agree that there is currently
a book on my desk, that there are many books in the Library of Congress, and that the Bible is a justifiably often-read book. It is in the
course of his philosophical investigations that a most interesting fact
about books is discovered—that, necessarily, they are objects that exist
in minds, that they cannot exist unperceived. Concomitantly, to Berkeley the term 'book', or the concept 'book', necessarily refers to a mental
entity or an idea. To claim that 'books exist [or even can exist] independent of being perceived', is to express nothing less than a (logical)
contradiction. In short, to Berkeley part of the meaning of 'book' is 'an
object that must be perceived by a mind'.

Yet some argue that it is part of the meaning of 'book'—that it is
intrinsic to the concept 'book'—to refer to objects that do, or at least
can, exist independent of any mind. So Berkeley's "agreement" with us
that the Library of Congress contains many books is misleading, for
although our word and Berkeley's are homonymous, they have distinct
connotations. To avoid confusion, Berkeley should have coined a new
term, 'i-book', say, to emphasize that his 'books' are necessarily objects
in persons' minds. On this rendering of Berkeley, he is to be classified as
a revisionist in that, contrary to his avowals, he is introducing a new
terminology and a radical metaphysics.

We can situate this debate in a currently fashionable lexicon. If we
assume that the truth conditions of a proposition determine the proposition's meaning (i.e., tell us what concepts are being used), what we want
to know is whether a partial catalog of the truth conditions of

there are many books in the Library of Congress

includes the ontological status of books. That is, we want to know if part of what makes the proposition true is the mind-dependent or mind-independent nature of books. If the ontological status *is* essential to the proposition's truth conditions (and thus, by assumption, to its meaning), then Berkeley does seem to mean something different than most of us mean when he talks about 'books'; that is, Berkeley's philosophy is revisionist. If, however, the ontological status is *not* essential to the proposition's truth-value (and thus, by assumption, inessential to its meaning), Berkeley can be viewed as using 'book' as we typically do; that is, Berkeley is engaging in descriptive metaphysics and has made a very interesting discovery concerning our ordinary use of language and the makeup of our conceptual scheme. On this rendering, Berkeley has elucidated and not invented.

How is this question to be resolved? How are we to determine whether Berkeley is elucidating our ordinary concepts or inventing a new technical vocabulary? When we consult the dictionary, the codification of our ordinary usage, we find that the definition of 'book' makes no reference to books' ontic status. It is not part of the definition of 'book' that it exist either mind-dependently or mind-independently. One might be tempted, then, to describe Berkeley's work as elucidation or description, confirming what Berkeley took himself to be doing, for the omission of any ontic significance from the definition of the term certainly suggests that its ontic status is not essential to its meaning. But enthusiasm for this descriptivist verdict should be tempered. Those who view Berkeley as a technical revisionist will reply that the existence of a pervasive realist supposition makes superfluous, if not perverse, any reference to a book's ontological status. Even Berkeley would heartily agree that there is a difference in kind, and not merely in degree, between a 'real' book and, say, a dreamt one, and yet there is no indication in the dictionary definition that the concept of book includes 'reality'. Furthermore, advocates of the revisionist rendering will claim it is hardly surprising that such a widely accepted supposition, which could be challenged only by a philosopher, should remain inexplicit.

Perhaps a more productive strategy is to ask the general populace whether they would still consider those objects that line the shelves in the Library of Congress *books* if those objects had existence only in the minds of persons. Would they still call such items 'books'? My experience, and it is obviously rather limited and selective, is that, presented with this revelation, they would now deny the existence of books rather than maintaining that books still exist only with a radically different nature than they had previously thought. What this suggests is that our concept of 'book', what we take to be a book, is inconsistent with an ontology radically at odds with our commonsense realist framework. (This hardly shows that our concepts are inelastic; it merely demonstrates that there are limits to their flexibility.) By this measure, his protestations to the contrary, Berkeley is engaging not in articulating our ordinary language, but in manufacturing a novel, technical vocabulary.

3.6   Armed with a keener awareness of the significance, in philosophical disputes, of the difference between articulating and creating, and having at least a rough idea how to ascertain, in an individual case, which activity a philosopher is engaging in, let us return to the compatibility problem.

It has seemed to many virtually platitudinous that the happenings in our world are bound to occur (are necessitated, determined), given the way the world was just before the event in question, along with the ways the world operates. So, for example, given that I am just about to release a ball from five feet above a table and that our world operates in such a way that objects so released fall, it seems that any other result than the ball hitting the table when it is dropped is absolutely ruled out. If we call 'ways the world is' 'states of the world', and 'ways the world operates' 'laws of nature', we have this commonsense position of determinism as claiming that any event that occurs must occur, given its antecedent state of the world and the laws of nature. Niceties aside, this very plausible-sounding doctrine has been characterized in the following three, essentially equivalent, formulations:

(1) For any event E, there is some set of past circumstances that, when conjoined with the laws of nature, logically suffices for the occurrence of E.

(2) If event E occurs in one logically possible world, W, then E occurs in every logically possible world that shares the past circumstances and laws of nature of W.

(3) If p and q are propositions that express the state of the world at some instants (q expressing a later moment than p), then p conjoined with the propositions denoting the laws of nature entails q.

I believe it is fair to grant to the participants in the compatibilist problem that (1), (2), and (3) constitute articulations (elucidations, precise formulations) of our ordinary concept of 'determinism'. Indeed, these statements are models of what good articulations should be. The justification for this concession to those participating in the debate is, again, merely an investigation of the way language is used. When people are offered an explanation of (1), (2), or (3), they agree (at least, once again, in my limited experience) that these formulations capture what they mean when they use the term 'determine', at least insofar as events are said to be determined (or settled, bound, or decided).

I certainly do not want to give the impression that an argument cannot be mustered that (1), (2), and (3) are revisionist renderings of 'determine'. But for the sake of my strategy, at least, I can grant that 'determinism' is not used in some technical sense that fails to capture the meaning attributed to it when persons reflect about a possible conflict between determinism and free will. At any rate, even if one believes this concession is unwarranted, it is worthwhile to see just how powerful an argument can be provided for the insubstantivity of the compatibilist problem if we focus solely on the concept of 'free will'.

Let us turn now to (ii), the claim that persons have free will. Much like (i), this claim is supposed to strike us as a platitude, as a claim that is part and parcel of our everyday, ordinary way of conceptualizing the world. However, we rarely make use of the expression 'free will', unlike the rather frequent use of 'determine'. On the rare occasions when we do use it ('he went to the doctor of his own free will'), it seems, to my ear at least, somewhat strained and usually just a cumbersome way of expressing voluntary action. Apparently this equivalence cannot be correct—philosophers of freedom are fond of distinguishing between free-willed and voluntary actions. At any rate, these reflections are not fatal to the view that we have an ordinary concept of free will; it may just be that such an ordinary concept is usually expressed by terminology other than 'free will'.

We should receive some help from the dictionary.[6] For 'free will' we have "freedom of decision or of choice between alternatives; the freedom of the will to choose a course of action without external coercion but in accordance with the ideals or moral outlook of the individual." For 'free' we find "not under the control of some other person or arbitrary power; able to act or think without compulsion or arbitrary restriction; not restricted by anything except its own limitations or nature." Thus if 'free will' is to be countenanced as an ordinary concept, one would need to understand it as more or less equivalent to

(FW)   being able to choose (decide) between alternative courses of action in a manner unrestricted by anything other than the individual's own nature.

The question now becomes whether philosophers of freedom have been using this ordinary concept of 'free will' while participating in the compatibilist problem. Obviously, not every such participant can be inventoried. I will use Hume as my representative compatibilist and van Inwagen as my representative incompatibilist. Although poles apart on the answer to the compatibility problem, both share the virtue of clarity, especially on the issue we are concerned with.

First Hume:

(H)   By liberty ['free will'], then, we can only mean *a power of acting or not acting, according to the determinations of the will*; that is, if we choose to remain at rest, we may; if we choose to move, we also may. ([35], his emphasis)

86

Notice that Hume takes himself to be elucidating our ordinary concept of free will. This is obvious not only from his wording in H ('we can only mean'), but even from a cursory examination of "On Liberty and Necessity," from which H is excerpted. Yet, as we have already seen in the case of Berkeley, this hardly suffices as proof for what Hume actually does.

The major conflict between H and FW is their differing conceptions concerning the locus of freedom—where free will is situated. According to FW, free will is either present or absent in the choice (or decision), whereas to H free will is placed subsequently, in the action according with the choice of decision. Hume in particular, and compatibilists in general, has been chastised for this putative misplacement. The complaint is often put in rhetorical terms: if the choice is determined by factors over which the individual has no control, then surely the person lacks free will even though H is satisfied. The point frequently is picturesquely exemplified by alluding to an unwitting individual whose mind is manipulated by a hypnotist (or neurosurgeon or evil demon) so that he now makes certain choices and then acts appropriately (later, such a scenario will reappear in more detail).

The present criticism is similar but nonetheless importantly distinct from this traditional one. No longer need we debate whether these strange scenarios involving these malevolent agents make conceptual sense or whether these anti-Humean thought experiments are really as telling as they appear. The point now is that H, Hume's account of 'freedom', is not an account of the ordinary notion of freedom that is basic to the reflective yet prephilosophical origins of the compatibility problem. Hume is not the descriptivist he takes himself to be.

3.7   Let us turn now to Peter van Inwagen, our representative incompatibilist.

When I say of a man that he 'has free will' I mean that very often, if not always, when he has to choose between two or more mutually incompatible courses of action—that is, courses of action that it is impossible for him to carry out more than one of—

each of these courses of action is such that he can, or is able to, or has it within his power to carry it out. A man has free will if he is often in positions like these: he must now speak or now be silent, and he *can* now speak and *can* now remain silent; he must attempt to rescue a drowning child or else go for help, and he is *able* to attempt to rescue the child and *able* to go for help; he must now resign his chairmanship or else lie to the members, and he has it within his power to resign and he has it within his power to lie. ([79], 8)

For van Inwagen, then, 'free will' is to be understood in terms of 'can' (or 'power to act' or 'being able to act'). It seems that van Inwagen attaches freedom to actions, not to choices and decisions, and so like Hume he would be subject to the charge that he is not employing the ordinary sense. This, though, would be hasty; perhaps the use of 'can' or 'being able to' that van Inwagen attaches to actions entails the ordinary sense of 'being able to' that FW attaches to actions and decisions. At the very least we need to understand how van Inwagen is using 'can' and its variants.

But how is 'can' to be defined? I am afraid I do not know how to define 'can' any more than I know how to define 'law of nature.' Nevertheless, I think that the concept expressed by 'can' in the examples given in the preceding paragraph [the one excerpted above]—the concept of the power or ability of an agent to act—is as clear as any philosophically interesting concept is likely to be. In fact, I doubt very much whether there are any simpler or better understood concepts in terms of which this concept might be explained. ([79], 9)

Van Inwagen then continues to distinguish his use of 'can' from other uses. His 'can' is not that of legal or moral responsibility, physical possibility, epistemic possibility, causal power, capacity, or skill (accomplishment).[7]

This is an unsettling situation. It is unsettling *not* because van Inwagen's use of 'can' cannot be understood in 'simpler or better understood terms' (for surely if this were the criterion for a successful explication, no explication would ultimately be satisfying), but because no lexical account suffices for our understanding of this allegedly ordinary, nontechnical word. The appeal to cases (e.g., we must either speak or remain silent, and we can speak and can remain silent) as the sole source of our understanding of the concept expressed by van Inwagen's 'can' will leave him in a most embarrassing position.

3.8 Paradigm case arguments are arguments that are meant to demonstrate the necessary correctness of a particular use of language. That is, there are certain situations—ideal situations, one might say—in which we cannot help but be correct; for example, in claiming there is a book before us or that there is a clock on the wall. If such argumentation is valid, powerful antiskeptical results seem to follow; at least a general skepticism concerning the existence of a material world no longer appears viable. We no longer need be concerned about whether it is possible that we will always be wrong about our existence claims concerning books, because the very meaning of 'book' is fixed by certain perceptions we have in particular situations. Roughly, then, to try to doubt the truth of 'there is currently a book before me' when the conditions include a healthy perceiver having book perceptions while observing an object in perfect sunlight and in no way obscured is to engage in a necessarily self-defeating activity. The sense of 'book' is determined (that is just what we mean by 'book') by having such perceptions in such situations. No skeptical wedge can enter because paradigm case arguments, if successful, show that in some instances language and experience are contiguous.

This type of argument has lost its currency. The basic skeptical rebuttal can be picturesquely put in terms of the machinations of an evil demon. Perhaps an evil demon is systematically presenting us with book illusions, identical in appearance to real books but without any paper or ink. In such a scenario we would be making a mistake in claiming to see a book in our rooms, or even in believing that there are books at all, although if we knew nothing of the evil demon's existence, we might well be justified in these most mundane of statements. Such considerations are used to show that regardless of the quality of our perceptions or observations, we can never have the logical security of a particular ontology. We cannot infer "there are books" from "this is just what we call (mean by) 'books'." Van Inwagen effectively agrees with this rebuttal ([79], 106–13).

Like all arguments or rebuttals to arguments, this skeptical rejoinder rests on suppositions. The key supposition, for our purposes, is that there are criteria for being a book that are independent of our sense perceptions for what we normally take as books. These criteria are not difficult to find. My dictionary offers as the meaning of 'book', "a number of sheets of paper, parchment, etc. with writing or printing in them, fastened together along one edge, usually between protective covers." The point here is not that we cannot, with some imagination, create entities that we would claim are books although they are not in complete concurrence with the definition (perhaps, for example, some written pages fastened along two edges), but rather that the criteria for being a book are logically independent of any of our perceptions. This gives us the logical space between cases and criteria that the skeptic requires to insert his rebuttal.

If this is an accurate view of the dialectical situation, paradigm case argumentation would be most persuasive where there is little or no logical space between cases and criteria. I think there are such cases, most perspicuously involving colors. To see this, we need to examine what would occur if the skeptical strategy were iterated with, for example, the color yellow. Here the evil genius putatively is systematically deceiving us into believing that the color we call 'yellow', thus called because we have a certain visual sensation, really is not yellow. The skeptic suggests that if he were to remove the illusory veneer around all these objects, we would all see that these objects were not yellow, but blue.

The success of this skeptical ploy is contentious. It is not implausible to understand yellow as just that color that we normally perceive when viewing gold, butter, or ripe lemons. If we understand yellow in just this way, then the gap between criteria and cases seems to vanish, because the way things are normally perceived is unaffected by its being illusory.

However, one might plausibly offer an "angstrom unit" definition of yellow ('yellow is that color that is *x* angstroms'), in which case there is no logically necessary connection between yellow and how it appears. For our purposes we need not delve into all the various ramifications (e.g., Are these both accounts of the same concept?). I wish only to point out that there are some examples where paradigm case argumentation is at least plausible.

Let us now return to van Inwagen's discussion of free will. Van Inwagen provides the following imaginary case in an attempt to point out the ineffectiveness of paradigm case argumentation.

> If we should discover that some particular person—Himmler, say—acted as he did because a Martian device [van Inwagen's analogue of our evil genius] implanted in his brain at the moment of his birth [undetectable by any observational technique we have now, though not in principle undetectable] had caused all his decisions, then we should hardly want to say that Himmler had free will, that he could have helped what he did, that he had any choice about the way he acted, or that he ever could have done otherwise. And I don't see why matters should be different if we discovered that everyone was "directed" by a Martian device: Then we should have to make these judgments about everyone. ([79], 110)

Although various pertinent questions can be asked about such a scenario, let us allow the conclusion that van Inwagen reaches—that we would deny free will to Himmler. The problem, however, is that van Inwagen's approach to the understanding of 'can' leaves this conclusion mysterious. If we ask ourselves why we believe Himmler lacks free will, the answer seems to be that his decisions are restricted or limited by something other than his nature. This coincides with our ordinary notion of free will, a notion that is lexically codified. But without this criterion of free will, or any other for that matter, and relying exclusively on *cases* (exemplars or paradigms), it seems capricious, if not mysterious, why we would have any inclination to deny Himmler's free will. Van Inwagen's account of free will parallels the antiskeptic's case for yellow that understood the color as that color perception we have when we see gold, bananas, or ripe lemons. This was precisely the type of situation where paradigm case argumentation has its greatest plausibility. Thus van Inwagen finds himself in a rather uncomfortable situation: his refusal to allow any satisfactory lexical account of 'free will' and his concomitant insistence that attention to cases provides the only explication of the concept commit him to the validity of a type of argument he explicitly rejects. Van Inwagen, being a libertarian, believes that persons have free will but clearly rejects the notion that this can be demonstrated by appeal to paradigm case considerations. Yet it is just this notion that he is coerced to accept, given his way of accounting for his 'free will' terminology.

3.9   If the foregoing considerations are at least right-headed, the free will issue is problematic essentially because of the lack of agreement concerning 'free will' or 'can'. This is not a platitudinous result. As a matter of fact, I must admit some residual uneasiness in laying the whole of the trouble at the door of the 'free will' component while leaving the 'determinism' contribution guiltless. It is rare in philosophy when the key terms in a problem do not, at least to some extent, share the blame. (Consider, for example, the terms 'universal' and 'particular' when used in the debate concerning universals.) Nonetheless, this is the conclusion I am led to accept.

Compatibilists, by and large, define freedom conditionally.[8] Such an analysis, as we have seen, is highly problematic. Incompatibilists (at least libertarians) generally offer an unconditional, categorical account of freedom. The sense of 'freedom' is given by examples, but this requires acceptance of paradigm case argumentation, a type of reasoning that, at least generally, is suspect. If the 'can' of human agency really does have content beyond causal power, causal capacity, physical possibility, and so forth, it is not clear that incompatibilists have given anything like a clear account of what this content amounts to. Until one is forthcoming, or until conditional analyses are vindicated, it seems difficult to see how any headway can be made concerning the compatibility problem.[9] Furthermore, this leads to the rather disappointing result that, as of now at least, discussions of the compatibility problem have no, or very little, impact on the issue of metaphysical fatalism. We simply do not gain any insight into the nature of past necessity from a problem that contains equivocal and mysterious notions of necessity. Though it is deflating, one might garner some satisfaction from a certain irony: the seriousness with which philosophers treat the compatibility problem and perfunctoriness with which these same philosophers typically treat fatalism may be examples of attitudes misplaced.

FOUR

FATALISM AND MORAL RESPONSIBILITY

4.1 Metaphysical fatalism claims that all events occur with the necessity of past events. Logical fatalism tells us that all events occur with logical necessity. What is the relation of these doctrines to the commonsense belief that some of us, at least some of the time, are morally responsible for some of our actions?

The consensus, if not unanimity of opinion, has it that fatalism in either of its guises is antithetical to our ordinary belief. More precisely, fatalism is said to entail that at no time are any of us morally responsible for any of our actions. The skeleton of such an argument is straightforward: moral responsibility requires freedom; fatalism is incompatible with freedom; and so fatalism precludes moral responsibility. Indeed, many view such a consideration as ringing the death knell for any form of fatalism. Since we cannot (for either logical, pragmatic, or intuitive reasons) sacrifice our belief in moral responsibility, fatalism's falsity is (logically, pragmatically, or intuitively) ensured. This same sort of reductio is frequently found in the literature concerning the free will–determinism issue. Here it is first argued that there is incompatibility between determined acts and moral responsibility for such acts. It is then stated—and now we can take our pick—as 'obvious', 'logically mandated', 'pragmatically guaranteed', 'conceptually assured', and the like, that we are in general morally responsible for our actions. Thus it is vouchsafed that determinism is false. It would not be surprising if points of contact between the antideterminism and antifatalism arguments emerged in the development of our discussion.

4.2   The thesis that moral responsibility requires freedom is one that, until recently, has been shrouded in an aura of dogmatic inviolability. Most frequently enunciated in terms of " 'ought' implies 'can'," the thesis has characteristically been viewed as a self-evident truth unquestioned by philosophers or by the ordinary person on the street. Some have even claimed that the source of the self-evident status resides in the nature of morality itself, that there is a conceptual relation between the type of enterprise or activity that constitutes morality and our ability to perform actions for which we are legitimately held responsible.

The principle itself is typically put to use in cases where one tries to demonstrate that it is unwarranted to blame someone for failing to perform a particular act, since in the given circumstances the individual in question was unable to or could not perform the action he failed to perform. Though it is normally implemented in cases like these, such cases do not clearly articulate the intuition behind the principle. If the cause of our inability to perform a particular action at a particular time is itself a product of previous actions that were under our control, then our present inability does not in itself exempt us from being morally responsible at this time. Such a consideration does not require that we relinquish " 'ought' implies 'can'," but simply has us understand the 'can' as being fulfilled *somewhere* along the causal etiology of the act in question and not necessarily being satisfied at the moment the person fails to perform the act. (This idea will be elucidated later.)

A second point about this principle is that it becomes moot if the individual actually performs the act in question. Alternatively put, this principle that concerns a necessary condition for warranted ascription of moral responsibility is relevant only when the agent fails to perform the act in question. If an agent actually performs a particular action, then he can perform that action, and so the necessary condition for moral responsibility is satisfied. Indeed, this claim concerning the relation between the actual performance of an action and the ability to perform it is taken as so obvious that *any* analysis of 'can' that is incompatible with 'the performance of p by S ensures S's ability to perform p' is taken to be woefully inadequate. This attitude is understandable. It is, after all, difficult to imagine a better proof of someone's ability to perform an action than his actually performing it.

Consider now a case where an individual must perform a particular action—where, that is, the individual cannot help but perform that action. One might argue that this is an illicit use of the term 'action', that the performance of an action requires that it be freely performed. Such a suggestion makes 'free action' a pleonasm, at least if we broadly interpret 'free', as we did previously, to mean action is considered free if the agent, somewhere along the act's causal etiology, has the ability to exercise this freedom. Let us forgo discussion of this essentially verbal point for one more germane. If an action is necessitated for an individual—if an individual necessarily performs some action—then he performs (tenselessly) that action. And from the trivial relation that obtains between agents' performance of actions and their abilities to perform them, it follows that agents can perform these necessitated actions. These actions thus pass the " 'ought' implies 'can' " test; that is, necessitated actions fulfill a necessary condition for holding their respective agents morally responsible.

It has seemed to many that agents who could not help but perform particular actions are not to be held morally responsible for their performance. We seem to require, then, a restriction on the legitimate ascription of moral responsibility to agents concerning the actions they actually perform. Thus, such a restriction is applicable to cases that trivially fulfill the necessary condition laid down by the " 'ought' implies 'can' " principle. The principle that articulates this restriction has been dubbed the "principle of alternate possibilities" (PAP; cf. [22]).

(PAP)   An agent is morally responsible for what he has done (for the action he has performed) only if he could have done otherwise (could have performed an action distinct from the one he actually performed).

A small industry has emerged of discussing PAP, with the consensus that, strictly speaking, PAP is false but that modifications or alternatives can be found to replace the deficient principle while maintaining the insight PAP tried to capture. It will be instructive to summarize some of the maneuvering so we can gain a clearer picture of the import of PAP.

Frankfurt's original counterexample to PAP spoke of Black's wanting Jones to perform an act and being willing and able to force Jones to perform that act if he does not do so out of his own preference and inclination. Supposing Jones knows nothing of Black's intentions and abilities and does perform the act in question of his own accord, it seems correct to attribute moral responsibility to Jones for his action. Thus we have a case where Jones could not do otherwise than perform the act in question and yet, since his action was a result of his own preference and inclination, he is justifiably held morally responsible for it. What we apparently have, then, is a case of preemptive causation. Jones's action was actually a product of his own preference and inclination, a psychology developed normally and noncoercively. However, had this psychology not been effective in motivating Jones to perform the particular act Black wanted performed, Black, using coercive techniques, would have forced Jones to perform it anyway.

Of course, for this putative counterexample to PAP to be successful, then, minimally, the action that constitutes what Jones actually does needs to be identical to the action that constitutes what Jones would do if Black's coercive techniques came into play. This obviously brings in difficult questions, for not only do we need to know something about the identity conditions of actions, we also need some knowledge about their transworld identity conditions.[1] Many philosophers would argue that we have here a case of distinct motivating factors and therefore distinct actions that result from these factors. They would argue that if there are different causes of a person's performing an act, the acts so performed cannot be identical. In Frankfurt's case this caveat seems to apply, for the actual world contains an action motivated by the agent's own preference and inclination, while the counterfactual case includes an action by the agent induced by the coercion of another. Indeed, it might be thought perverse to consider the counterfactual case even an example of an action. One might reasonably argue that the performer in this case merely behaves rather than acts, and that to identify mere behavior with action is to conflate what should be separated. It is often commented that the ability to act rather than the mere capability of behaving is one of the major differences between minded entities and mindless ones.

These considerations, though, hardly settle the matter. Suppose Black's coercive techniques resulted in Jones's coming to have a psychology of preferences and inclinations that were, so to speak, episodically identical to the psychology that he actually did own and that actually was efficacious. Here the content and strength of the preference and inclination in the counterfactual case would be congruent with the content and strength of the preferences of the psychology the agent has in the actual world. If we are still wont to claim that the two psychologies are distinct, the distinctness would have to be based on different etiologies. Thus the central question now, under the assumption that distinct psychologies suffice for distinct actions, is whether different causal histories mandate distinct psychologies. We need, then, to offer a satisfying account of the identity conditions of the items making up our mental life—a task that at the very least is daunting.

These points, as well as others, emerge in the context of an example of David Blumenfeld's. His purportive counterexample to PAP has us supposing that

> the presence of a certain atmospheric reaction always causes Smith to decide to attack the person nearest to him and to actually do so. Suppose also that he always flushes a deep red when he considers and decides against performing an act of violence and that under certain circumstances the atmospheric reaction is triggered by the appearance of just this shade of red. Now imagine that on a day on which circumstances are favorable to the triggering of the reaction, Smith considers whether or not to strike a person with whom he is conversing, decides in favor of it, and forthwith does so. ([9], 341)

Such an example purportedly has advantages over Frankfurt's original, unadorned case of Jones and Black. Here, unlike Frankfurt's case, both the actual and counterfactual events are motivated (caused) by the agent's own decisions. This can be seen as a way of trying to obviate the earlier major criticism cast in terms of either an illicit conflation of action with mere behavior or an illicit identification of actions that are distinctly motivated. In Blumenfeld's case both the actual and counterfactual events are *actions,* since roughly they are caused by mental events. Moreover, they are claimed to be identical actions, since the behaviors caused by the decisions are identical. So, allegedly, we now have an uncontentious counterexample to PAP, since the agent ought to be held morally responsible for his attack even though he could not have done other than perpetuate this attack—where the attack is now understood as essentially containing both a particular behavior and a prior mental state.

But once again this is hardly conclusive. Surely what catches our attention and deserves scrutiny is the idea that an atmospheric reaction causes our decision to attack. There are two ways of turning this bizarre scenario against Blumenfeld. One might argue that "decisions" need be brought about in rather standard ways in order for us to countenance them as (real) decisions and that, perhaps, although what constitutes a "standard way" is rather vague, introducing a "decision" via an atmospheric reaction falls inadmissibly outside even such a rough-hewn border. Alternatively, one might allow that in both the actual and counterfactual cases the agent does make a (real) decision (and thus sidesteps what may be construed as a mere verbal issue) but now (a) either claim that the decisions, and therefore the actions, are not identical in the actual and counterfactual cases, since the etiology of a decision is essential to its nature, or (b) allow that the decisions per se are identical in both cases, yet require the identical actions have not only congruent behaviors and decisions but congruent (or nearly congruent) causal histories. Relying on either (a) or (b) allows the proponent of PAP to resist Blumenfeld's example, for it permits a denial of what is required of such a counterexample—that *what the agent does* (the action) is identical in the actual and counterfactual cases.

4.3   The plausibility that PAP initially has depends, as did the plausibility of the " 'ought' implies 'can' " principle, on understanding the temporal scope of 'could have done otherwise' as extending backward throughout the relevant causal history of the agent. To see this, consider the case of a man who imbibes too heavily at a party. After several vodkas, he can no longer help screaming at his blond host. That is, let us assume that it is a natural necessity that if a person with the genetic makeup of Bob drinks the quantity of liquor Bob drank in a specified time, he will scream at the first blond person he sees. Still, we would not, I believe, morally exculpate Bob for his rude behavior if we further believed that it was 'up to him' whether to drink as much as he did. The intuition here is that since Bob was free to avoid putting himself in a situation in which he no longer had any control, he should be held morally accountable for his actions.

This intuition is apparently strengthened by considering the case of Frank, who develops alcoholism while still a fetus in his mother's womb (unfortunately, such a horrible scenario can and does occur). For our purposes, we can say that such a condition is tantamount to having an 'irresistible inclination' to drink alcohol. At the party Frank can do no other than drink and, assuming he has the same genetic makeup as Bob, can therefore do no other than scream at the first blond he sees.

In such a case is Frank to be held morally accountable for his rude behavior? Although it is true, ex hypothesi, that he cannot help drinking and the he cannot help screaming at a blond once he is drunk, one might still argue that he was not compelled to go to the party in the first place. If he knew what his behavior was likely to be at the party and attended anyway, then he should be held morally accountable. Or one might argue that Frank could have tried to get help for his alcoholism, perhaps by seeking psychological counseling or attending Alcoholics Anonymous meetings. Since he did not, it is proper to consider him morally blameworthy for his behavior at the party.

As in the case of Bob, it seems that freedom, somewhere along the causal ancestry of the action, is necessary to justify ascribing moral responsibility. It seems required that *somewhere* along the line culminating in the intentional action, it must be "up to" the agent in order for moral accountability to be warranted. Furthermore, to both Frankfurt and Blumenfeld the inclination to consider the agents morally responsible seemed to require that the actual course of events include a "free" decision. Reflecting on the case where not only does someone not know about his likely future behavior, but this privation of knowledge is brought about by factors over which he could have no say (no decision by the agent could have mattered, as a matter of empirical necessity, to the outcome), seems to result in an exculpatory verdict. We have certainly seen just this type of thinking exemplified in recent presidential politics. Claims of "being out of the (information) loop," supported by proclamations that such situations are "normal," are "natural," and "expedite the running of government" are supposed to be seen by the public as valid excuses, cleansing the political actors involved of any tinge of sin.

Finally, consider the case of Harry, who is about to act in accordance with his (free) decision to slap his landlord ([65], 43). As he is about to move his arm forward, William, a neurophysiologist, manipulates a machine so that it blocks the neuromuscular activity necessary for Harry's action to be carried out as a product of Harry's decision making. Simultaneously, William pushes Harry's arm into his landlord's face at precisely the same position and with the same force that it would have had, had Harry's intention been allowed to function normally.

Notice that this case differs from both Frankfurt's and Blumenfeld's. In the former two cases the agent's action actually came about through a freely formed motivational structure. Here the action comes about through a factor not under the agent's control, though its result was intended and presumably would have occurred had the neurophysiologist not interfered. Here many people share the intuition that Harry is morally responsible for slapping his landlord and, moreover, has the same degree of moral accountability as had his freely formed intention not been thwarted. Here it is suggested that there is no relevant locus of freedom in the causal ancestry of the act, and so PAP is demonstrably false.

One way of defending PAP is to argue that in such a case the moral accountability attaches to Harry's intent and not his subsequent action. On this account we do not blame Harry for slapping his landlord (this slapping, one might argue, is no more an action of Harry's than is an unexpected spasm); rather, we blame him for the type of person he is—for the character traits he has allowed himself to develop. Such an explanation once again carries with it the presumption that Harry had it "in his power" to not develop, or at least to control, his untoward behavior. By failing to exercise this ability, Harry has become the sort of man we morally disapprove of. On this rendering of the scenario, then, PAP seems unaffected, since there is no *action* for which we hold Harry morally responsible.

This is probably not, I think, understood as a case of someone's meaning to do something and doing it, but not in the way the agent intended. It is not, that is, best classified as an action deviantly caused. The content of Harry's intention is not merely that his arm hit his landlord. Rather, his intention consists of a "de se" content that he himself should slap his landlord's face. We would need to know more details of Harry's psychology for a clear verdict, but it seems eminently plausible that Harry would feel less than fully satisfied by the result of William's manipulations. His complaint that "I wanted to do it" would be quite intelligible in such a context. This, of course, is not to say that Harry would be completely unhappy with the ensuing state of affairs; but Harry's glee concerning his landlord's newly acquired bruise might be tempered.

This, then, is a brief sketch, along with some comments, about the recent literature concerning the principle of alternate possibilities, which holds that a person's ability to do otherwise (freedom) is essential for any justified ascription of moral responsibility. To my mind, then, no decisive argument or illustration has been so far forwarded that coerces us to retract or diminish our faith in the intuition PAP expresses.

4.4   Whereas Frankfurt's article has been the source of one contemporary debate concerning the relation between moral responsibility and freedom, Julia Driver's article has been another ([14]). In this article she formulates a paradox of promising:

(1)   Whenever a person makes a promise to do x, he thereby puts himself under an obligation to do x.

(2) If someone is obligated to do x, then he can do x.

(3) Some people make promises they cannot keep.

This is a paradox because though each of these propositions by itself has great initial plausibility, they are jointly inconsistent. Since the articulation of the paradox, A. P. Martinich and Walter Sinnott-Armstrong have engaged in a debate about the best means of resolution, with Martinich opting for a rejection of (3) while Sinnott-Armstrong suggests that (2) be dismissed (cf. [48], [49], [67]). For our purposes it is the latter rejection that holds most interest, for rejecting (2) is tantamount to rejecting the " 'ought' implies 'can' " principle. It will be worthwhile to delve into this debate in some detail, as it was to examine the dialogue concerning PAP. Afterward, our comments concerning the relation between fatalism and moral responsibility will be better informed.

Sinnott-Armstrong considers the following case:

> Suppose I say "I promise to drive you to the airport" even though I know that my only car does not work, and I know that you think it does. . . . Now suppose (albeit unlikely) that the mechanic finishes my car early, so that when the time comes, I can drive you to the airport. It is obvious that I would then have an obligation to drive you to the airport, if you still want a ride. ([67], 79)

Sinnott-Armstrong sees this as an example of a promise—and therefore, by (1), an obligation—to do something that a speaker cannot do. But why can't he do it? The car, thanks to the speedy mechanic, is available, though, one must admit, after the promise was uttered. But as Martinich correctly points out, the time a promise is uttered (and so the time when an obligation is incurred) need not be identical to the time when the obligation must be satisfied or dispatched. (Sinnott-Armstrong himself says that when the time comes he *can* drive to the airport.) The satisfied promise, unlike the articulation of the promise, lacks temporal specificity; however, some temporal borders are implied. One must, for example, drive the promisee early enough to catch his plane.

Although Martinich's point is conclusive against Sinnott-Armstrong's description of the case, we can add some details to make a decision more arguable. Consider a case where the promiser did not know that his car had been fixed prematurely. In this scenario, is it still proper to claim that he *can* drive the promisee to the airport? An affirmative answer is likely to be supported by pointing out that, given likely access to a phone, the promiser could have called the mechanic's shop and discovered that the car had been worked on earlier. Or even if a phone was for some reason inaccessible (there were no functioning ones available or the mechanic's shop had no phone), the promiser could have (assuming "normal" circumstances) walked to the shop to ask if the car was ready. It would be conceded that this idea normally would not occur to the promiser, and it might furthermore be conceded that, even under the auspices of his promise, such a course of action would not, in the circumstances, seem reasonable. Nonetheless, the issue here is what the promiser could have done, and he could have telephoned (or walked). Thus he could have known about the car and so could have brought it home in plenty of time to drive the promisee to the airport.

The general idea that appears to underlie this reasoning is that if an agent could bring about a certain state of affairs, and if these affairs are collectively sufficient (empirically) for the occurrence of a further state of affairs, then the agent could bring about this additional state of affairs. Here the agent could have telephoned his mechanic and discovered that his car would be home early enough for the drive. Telephoning the mechanic and bringing the car home suffice for his driving the promisee to the airport, and so the agent could fulfill the promise.

Yet a negative verdict, a verdict that the promiser could not drive the promisee to the airport, is also supportable. An apologist for this view will focus on the actual psychological state the promiser finds himself in and not on what he *could* do in such a situation. The emphasis is placed on the fact that the promiser does not know his car has already been fixed and firmly believes that it will not be functional for quite a while. The apologist does not deny that the agent could have made the telephone call; rather, he asserts that this ability is tangential to whether the promiser, in his state of ignorance, could have driven his friend to the airport. A bit more perspicuously, the intuition expressed here is that, given the promiser's firm belief that his car will not be ready until much later, he could not drive there. One might say that the promiser's mental condition prohibits him from fulfilling his promise. The position forwarded here is that although the promiser could perform certain events that would allow him to be able to fulfill his promise (in the sense that the psychological state that prohibits him from seeking out his automobile is not in any logical or empirical way necessitated), the fact that he could not perform those events (in the sense that, given his psychological state, it is empirically necessitated that he not take the otherwise possible steps to secure his car) is sufficient for the claim that he cannot fulfill his promise. 'Could', in this view, is not transitive or hypothetical.

The debate between the "categorical" and "hypothetical" viewpoints of 'could' is hardly new. Perhaps, however, we can cast the debate in a somewhat different light in hope of gaining some illumination. The "categorical" apologist, though denying that the promiser could have fulfilled his promise, may allow for the "hypothetical" apologist's insight by granting that the promiser had the ability to possess the ability to keep his promise. According to the categoricist, however, the meta-ability to perform a particular action does not suffice for the ability to perform such an action. Furthermore, the just attribution of moral responsibility depends on the agent's possessing an ability, and not a meta-ability, to perform a particular action. Thus the categoricist denies moral responsibility to the promiser despite his meta-ability to drive the promisee because he lacks the requisite ability. The hypotheticist—at least one who also accepts this casting of the distinction—apparently can forward his position in two ways. First, he may accept the view that the ability is what is necessary to the warranted ascription of moral responsibility, yet hold that possession of a meta-ability suffices for the possession of the lower-level ability. Taking this tack allows consensus concerning the interpretation of the " 'ought' implies 'can' " principle; the disagreement concerns what conditions suffice for the possession of an ability. The second avenue denies that the lower-level ability is what is necessary for moral responsibility. All that is necessary for the legitimate ascription of moral responsibility to an agent is that the agent have the meta-ability (or perhaps some even higher-order ability) to perform the act in question. In this view the higher-order ability does *not* suffice for the possession of a lower-order one. The general agreement on the "'ought' implies 'can'" principle that was reached previously now appears to break down.

In truth, these two tacks amount to much the same thing, for nothing mandates that one equate the lower-level ability with what one can do. That is, we can secure verbal agreement with the "'ought' implies 'can'" principle by identifying the meta-ability (or some even higher-level ability) with the condition necessary for the justified ascription of moral responsibility. This should not be surprising. Recent philosophy of language has questioned the validity of the putative distinction between the meaning of a term and the factors necessary for the term's correct application. The example at hand merely instantiates this skepticism; it is a moot point whether one agrees with the hypotheticist that the locus of freedom is found in the lower-level ability (although this requires the appropriate meta-ability) or whether one disagrees about where the freedom is situated (claiming that the meta-ability is the correct location) but concurs about the existence of freedom in any particular case.

Does it make any sense to speak of an ability to possess or gain another ability? And more to the point, does it make any sense or have any content beyond the simple ability to perform a certain action? One way to argue that such a notion has content is to give a convincing illustration where two persons lack the ability to perform a certain act and yet only one has the ability to gain that ability. Consider two ten-year-old boys, neither of whom has the strength and coordination necessary to consistently make twenty-five-foot jump shots. One is the progeny of two athletically gifted parents and will have the best training available, whereas the other is physically disabled with irreparable muscle and nerve damage to both of his arms. We now need to ask whether such a case is accurately described as one in which both ten-year-olds lack the ability to make twenty-five-foot jump shots while only the first has the ability to gain that ability.

It seems that such a case is inconclusive. Although there seems nothing to rule out such a description as legitimate, an adversarial position might hold that the difference between the two boys is best thought of as the possession and lack thereof of abilities as ten-year-olds. One boy at ten has the ability to perform such basketball feats at twenty, and the other boy lacks that ability. Such a line of thought, if pushed, would hold that we have at birth (and perhaps even earlier, depending on one's view of personhood) all the abilities to perform all the acts that we ever will perform. Any talk of additional, higher-order abilities is at best superfluous and at worst perverse.

Perhaps the point can be put even more starkly if we consider whether the development of a meta-ability drug is possible. Could we inject some people with a drug so that they would *gain* the ability to perform a particular action, or would the success of this injection simply mean they already had the ability to perform that action? It seems that the elasticity of the concept allows for either answer. We could say either that the injection brought about an ability the individual otherwise lacked or that the accomplishment of the physical feats after the injection is just evidence that the individual already had the ability.

If this train of thought is essentially correct, then the perennial debate concerning the "right" analysis of 'could' in 'could have done otherwise' is, if not much ado about nothing, then at least much ado about very little. The strategy employed to reach this result begins by mirroring this squabble in terms of a distinction between abilities and meta-abilities, and it is this distinction that has been shown to have little substance. It is open to hardened hypotheticists and categoricists to claim that in mirroring there has been distortion; that casting the perennial debate in these terms transmutes the problem into a historically unrecognizable issue, so that any illumination provided simply shines on an irrelevant area. This charge may be correct, since mirror images are never quite as crisp and pristine as the original. Nonetheless, the onus seems to lie with the debaters, who now need to show why the ability/meta-ability distinction does not capture the essence, much less the totality, of their dispute. At the very least, then, this discussion should force a needed clarity into the alleged distinction between the hypothetical and categorical 'could'.

108

If the strategy employed is basically right-headed, then the debate between Sinnott-Armstrong and Martinich concerning the validity of the "'ought' implies 'can'" principle loses much of its urgency. Or perhaps better put, the principle can be legitimately understood as articulating either a truth or a falsity without offending our moral intuition. The key substantive point that seems to emerge is that there must be a locus of freedom somewhere along the etiology of the individual's act.

Let us apply this machinery to two other cases that Sinnott-Armstrong creates as putative counterexamples to the "'ought' implies 'can'" principle. Consider a lifeguard who walks so far from his post that he cannot save drowning persons. Sinnott-Armstrong claims that this action cannot cancel his obligation to oversee the safety of the swimmers in his area ([67], 81).

But the reply is now obvious. Even if we grant that the lifeguard no longer can (has the ability to) save the drowning persons (a concession, as we have seen, that is hardly mandated), he had the meta-ability to save such persons. That is, he had the ability to have the ability to save such persons, for he had the ability not to leave his post. This is what is required for sustaining our intuition that the lifeguard is morally blameworthy if someone drowns in his sector.

Sinnott-Armstrong's second putative counterexample fares no better. He offers the illustration of a mother who has a moral obligation to care for a child she is not able to care for. One need only think of poverty-stricken women as examples of instantiating Sinnott-Armstrong's scenario ([67], 81).

But once again the rejoinder is that (even if once again we accept the description of such a woman as lacking the requisite ability) the woman had the ability to place herself in a situation where she did not suffer this disability. She could have, we can assume, simply abstained from sex. To see the force of this obvious reply, consider the case where such a woman was raped and did not have the ability to take steps to avoid such an attack. In this instance, I believe, the moral intuition for most of us changes. Here, where there is no locus of freedom, we feel that the woman does not have the moral obligation to care for the child. (This does not imply that the child has no right to be cared for.)[2]

4.5   In recent discussions of moral theory, the topic of moral dilemmas has gained prominence. One debate has concerned their reality, or lack thereof. Obviously the results of such an inquiry would have an impact on one's choice of a moral theory. If, for example, one concludes that there are, or at least could be, moral dilemmas, any moral theory that precludes even their possibility might well be dismissed a priori. But if one concludes that there are not and cannot be any moral dilemmas, then any theory that allows for their existence would have a rather formidable difficulty to overcome.

What, then, is a moral dilemma? For our purposes the following rough account will suffice: a moral agent finds himself in a moral dilemma if and only if he is in moral circumstances where he cannot perform an action he ought to perform. Thus the existence of moral dilemmas would prove fatal to the plausibility of "'ought' implies 'can'." As an example of such circumstances, consider an agent who promises both his father and his mother to drive them to their respective destinations at noon. Since his mother and father are to be quite distant from each other at noon, it seems clear that the son cannot keep both promises. But since each promise establishes an obligation, it appears we have a situation where someone has an obligation to perform an act he cannot perform. One might argue that if the son was aware at the time of his "promise" that his parents would be far apart and thus knew that fulfilling both promises would prove impossible, then the "promises" were infelicitous and so were null and void. On this view, although the son may have tokened the phrase 'I promise to . . .', no actual promise was made, for conditions necessary for making a promise are omitted (e.g., sincerity) (cf. [1] and [66]). To forestall pointless debates on whether insincere "promises" are (really) promises, let us assume that the agent's epistemic condition, along with all the conditions before noon, was identical to those that would have obtained had the ensuing conditions permitted the son to fulfill both promises.

The machinery developed may help us here as well. A necessary condition for moral responsibility is satisfied if, at any place along the etiology of the action, there is a locus of freedom for the agent. In the case under discussion, at least without further details to the contrary, the agent is morally responsible for his failure to fulfill his obligation. Whether this is tantamount to the " 'ought' implies 'can' " principle is, as we have seen, a verbal point.

PAP and the " 'ought' implies 'can' " principle are two articulations of a fundamental intuition concerning the relation between moral responsibility and freedom. We have seen how it is that we ought to understand these principles if we are to continue accepting them as true. In a somewhat extended sense, both of these principles may be maintained as linchpins of the just way persons should be judged for their actions.

We are now in a better position to investigate the nature of the relation between moral responsibility and fatalism. If we understand fatalism as logical fatalism, there is little to discuss. As we saw in some detail in chapter 1, logical fatalism, if true, is merely tautologically true. Assuming, as we implicitly have done, that PAP and " 'ought' implies 'can' " are substantive principles, it is difficult to discern what relevance can be found between these two very different sorts of statements. Indeed, any debate would seem perverse; a tautology or logical truth, whatever its verbal content, certainly cannot affect the character of any empirical claim. Those, then, who claim that our fundamental intuitions concerning the relation between moral responsibility and freedom provide *reasons* (indeed, conclusive reasons) against the tenability of fatalism, logically conceived, are under a misapprehension. Either they are misunderstanding the logical character of the type of fatalism they espouse, or they misunderstand what sorts of relations can hold between logical and empirical claims.

When we understand the doctrine of fatalism as metaphysical fatalism, we derive the benefit of an interesting question. Metaphysical fatalism, as an empirical and not a logical thesis, at least holds the possibility of having meaningful contact with our fundamental intuitions concerning moral responsibility and freedom. One might think that the relation is meaningful but obvious, that the correctness of even the extended versions of PAP and the " 'ought' implies 'can' " principle dictates the falsity of metaphysical fatalism. The argument is direct. Metaphysical fatalism is the view that all events occur with the necessity

111

of past events. As for our ability to affect or modify events, the future, present, and past are all on a par. Just as we believe we lack any ability to affect the past and therefore are precluded from having any moral responsibility toward past events, we likewise, given the truth of metaphysical fatalism, lack the ability to affect the constitution of the future and so are precluded from having any moral responsibility for the occurrence or nonoccurrence of those events. Justified ascription of moral responsibility and metaphysical fatalism are incompatible.

We may put the point slightly differently. PAP, even in its extended form, tells us that moral responsibility requires that the agent be able to have performed an act other than the one he actually performed. (Recall that the "extended" form does not demand that at the time when he performs the act in question he 'can' perform otherwise.) Of any past act we can neither now nor ever perform one in its stead. If metaphysical fatalism is true, then all acts have precisely this sort of necessity, and so alternative actions can never be undertaken. PAP therefore is unsatisfied, and moral responsibility cannot be legitimately ascribed to an agent for any of his actions. Similarly, the " 'ought' implies 'can' " principle, even in its extended form, requires the ability to perform an act as a condition of warranted moral responsibility. We cannot perform any past act and so cannot be held morally responsible for any past act. Since metaphysical fatalism imputes past necessity to all events, we would incur the same relation we have toward past events. Moral responsibility is therefore excluded in a metaphysically fated world.

There is one sophism that should be briefly addressed. One might suggest that all, or virtually all, of the actions I am held morally responsible for are past actions. Typically, if not universally, I am held morally responsible for things I have done and things I will do. Furthermore, the argument continues, such moral accountability is perfectly proper and justifiable. Since I can now do nothing to affect the constitution of the past, both the " 'ought' implies 'can' " principle and PAP are unsatisfied. Yet since the moral responsibility of the agent is in general warranted, both principles that putatively announce necessary conditions for the justified ascription or moral responsibility must be deemed false.

Accepting, arguendo, the claim that one can now do nothing about the past's constitution, the defenders of the two moral principles have an obvious rebuttal. A defender of PAP would claim that if I am now justifiably held responsible for my action of yesterday, it is in part because before yesterday's act I could have performed an act distinct from the one I actually did perform. An apologist of the "'ought' implies 'can'" principle would forward a similar idea by claiming that the very act I did perform yesterday shows that, yesterday, I could have performed that act.

Diagnosing the sophism's error is not difficult. It puts a burden on both PAP and the "'ought' implies 'can'" principle that they need not bear. This superfluous burden is constituted by assuming that the ability to perform an act distinct from the one actually performed (for PAP) and the ability to perform an act for which one has moral responsibility (for the "'ought' implies 'can'" principle) need be possessed by the agent at the time the moral responsibility is ascribed to him. But such a requirement entails a perverse understanding of the nature of both moral principles. As we have seen, taken in their extended senses, they necessitate only that the agent, at some time, have the abilities in question. The sophism, in effect, demands that the agent *always* have these abilities.

The question before us is whether there is any way it would be justifiable to hold a person morally responsible in a metaphysically fated world. Consider, in this context, the Lewis gambit. Although David Lewis initiated this strategy in the context of defending compatibil- ism—that is, of defending the possibility of freedom in a deterministic world—we might be able to transport his idea to a metaphysically fated world. Recall that although Lewis believes we cannot alter the past, he believes this inability is compatible with our ability to perform some action such that if that action were performed, the past would be differently constituted than had we not performed that action. The suggestion now is that if one is truly free to perform such a particular action, an avenue of reconciling metaphysical fatalism with justified ascriptions of moral responsibility may be opened.

To investigate whether such an idea can be exploited, let us once again concentrate on our relation to past events. If we can make sense of legitimate moral responsibility toward past events under the presupposition of past fatalism, we can automatically transport these ideas to the case of just attribution of moral responsibility to persons related to future events in a metaphysically fated world; for, after all, the type of necessity employed is precisely the same in both cases.

What is being envisioned is a world whose past consists of events P_1, P_2, and P_3. We are now in a position where one must perform either act F_1 or act F_2, where 'now in a position' amounts to 'having full freedom' to perform either of the alternative actions. Instantiation of the Lewis gambit has the realization that F_1, and F_1 alone, is correlated with P_4, and not P_1, that is, it is correlated with a slightly differently constituted past than the one that actually occurred in that world. The point seems to be that if the Lewis maneuver is intelligible, then there appears to be no violation of either the principle that " 'ought' implies 'can' " or PAP. To this extent, then, it is meaningful to speak of being morally responsible for the occurrence of past events. Since the free performance of F_1 is correlated with a past including P_4 and the free performance of F_2 is correlated with a past including P_1 (and not P_4), and since no violation occurs of the moral principles articulating necessary conditions or warranted responsibility, the onus now appears to shift to those who claim that justified ascription of moral responsibility to agents concerning past acts is absurd.

It should be emphasized that this Lewis gambit is distinct from PAP and so should not be thought of as offering a necessary condition for moral responsibility based on this principle. Recall that PAP tells us that a necessary condition for an agent's moral responsibility for an act is his ability to perform an alternative act. The Lewis gambit does not countenance applying PAP to a past event. It does not allow us to claim that given P_1, a past event, we are now able to perform not-P_1 in its stead. Rather, what it legitimizes is that we are now able to perform an act such that if we were to perform it, P_4 and not P_1 would form part of the past's constitution. The gambit is consistent with our inability to modify or undo the past; it allows us the ability to perform an act such that the past would contain one event rather than another. Consider my great-great-grandfather's cheating on his income tax. I cannot now undo or modify this event, if indeed this event actually occurred. But the gambit creates the possibility of my free performance of either of two actions such that if I do one, this cheating forms part of the actual past, whereas if I do the other it does not. To make the plausibility for moral accountability even stronger in this case, we can give the agent knowledge of the effects that would accrue from either choice. That is, the agent now knows that if and only if he performs a particular action, an action he is free to perform, his great-great-grandfather's cheating will occur.

Has some illicit maneuver slipped in? Obviously we should be skeptical, for we have reached a most counterintuitive result: it is sensible to hold persons morally accountable for past events. A range of bizarre stories now seems possible. Persons born thirty years ago are vilified for allowing World War I to occur. Present-day individuals are legitimately blamed for the exploits of Genghis Khan and Attila the Hun. And on the other side of the ledger, some current members of our society are praised for Lincoln's emancipation of the slaves and others for the medical discoveries of Pasteur.

One might argue that these possibilities demonstrate the absurdity of the Lewis gambit. That is, any strategy that permits even the possibility of an agent's being held responsible for a remotely past event no longer deserves serious consideration. But what is a reductio to one is a question-begging argument to another. It is difficult to see how such a reply would be forceful to those who are not already convinced of the gambit's inviability.

A more useful road might begin by reminding us of the two closely related principles concerning necessary conditions of moral responsibility—PAP and " 'ought' implies 'can'." PAP claims that a fundamental intuition concerning warranted attribution of moral responsibility makes necessary the ability to perform an act other than the one actually performed. If, after all, the gambit can be shown to be inconsistent with PAP—that is, if satisfaction of the gambit precludes PAP from being fulfilled—this would be, prima facie, a strong case against the viability of the gambit. To hold on to the gambit legitimizing moral responsibility of past events and yet gain such legitimacy at the cost of

115

preempting a powerful intuition concerning a necessary condition of moral responsibility would force the adherent of the gambit to modify or rescind altogether the intuition expressed by PAP.

It might seem that such an argument is easily forthcoming. The Lewis gambit legitimizes the possibility that the currently living Sam could justifiably be held morally responsible for the death of Lincoln. Yet Sam cannot alter the past; Lincoln's death cannot now be prevented by any action Sam can now perform. So, the argument concludes, if in fact the possibility permitted by the gambit is actualized, a violation of PAP occurs, and so the gambit's viability is eradicated.

One reply might take this objection as misfounded, as misconstruing the character of the gambit. Advocates of both the gambit and PAP agree (so we can assume, at least) that we cannot alter the past. What the gambit allows is that the performance of one free act is correlated with one past while the performance of another free act is correlated with a different past. Since there are two (at least) free acts the agent has available to him, this conforms with rather than violates PAP, which requires that the justified attribution of moral responsibility to the agent entail that the agent be able to perform otherwise. But the ability to perform otherwise is just what the gambit permits by speaking of free acts. What the gambit allows is that Lincoln's death would not have been past had Sam freely opted to perform a particular act. This grants Sam neither the power to change the past nor the ability to be held morally accountable for the performance of an unfree action.

The objector may not find this satisfying. PAP tells us that an agent can be legitimately held morally responsible for an act only if he can perform some other act. If Sam is to be held morally accountable for Lincoln's death, he would need to be able to prevent Lincoln's death. But as we all agree, arguendo, the past cannot be undone, and so PAP is after all violated and the gambit should be discarded, at least as it applies to cases of moral responsibility.

But the advocate of the Lewis gambit's moral applicability will point out that of course Sam did not shoot Lincoln (Booth did), and so even PAP does not require that he be able to, at any time, not shoot Lincoln. In fact, it is just the agreement between both parties that one cannot perform, modify, or undo a past that guarantees the consistency of PAP with the gambit's moral applicability. The inability an agent has regarding past events vouchsafes that these two ideas have no points of contact. PAP tells us that, if someone performs an act, moral responsibility occurs only if the agent could have done other than perform that act. But if the act is a past event, then both parties agree it is one that cannot be performed, let alone actually ever being performed. Thus PAP is not a principle that has application.

Matters are more difficult when we try to reconcile the Lewis gambit's moral applicability with the " 'ought' implies 'can' " principle, because of the essentially 'prospective' nature of this principle as opposed to the characteristically 'retrospective' nature of PAP. PAP deals with an action that an agent has performed. It requires, for legitimate ascription of moral responsibility, that the agent have had, at some time, the ability to perform a different act. PAP was unproblematic for the gambit's foray into the realm of moral responsibility because, arguendo, no past action is performable. The situation is reversed regarding the " 'ought' implies 'can' " principle. This principle requires that an individual be able to perform an action if moral responsibility is legitimately ascribed to the agent for that action. We do not, as in the case of PAP, already have an act that has been performed, for if we did, the necessary condition of moral responsibility stated by the " 'ought' implies 'can' " principle would be vacuously fulfilled. From the fact that the agent has already performed an act, it follows that he can perform that act (roughly, the possibility of x follows from its actuality), and so the actual performance of any act eo ipso dictates that its agent pass the necessary test of moral accountability laid down by the " 'ought' implies 'can' " principle.

With this background, it appears that a violation of the " 'ought' implies 'can' " principle is mandated if we are to hold an agent responsible for a remote past event. Since Sam cannot, at any time during his life, shoot Lincoln, adherence to the principle precludes Sam's being justifiably held morally responsible for shooting Lincoln. But since the gambit allows for legitimate accountability in such a case, its moral applicability must be denied.

117

There are various responses possible for those who wish to defend the Lewis gambit's moral applicability. The one I will suggest is, I think, intuitive, yet while consistent with the " 'ought' implies 'can' " principle, it forces us to understand the principle in a less superficial way.

First, it must be acknowledged that the following two abilities are not identical:

(a) The ability Sam now has to either shoot or not shoot Lincoln

(b) The ability Sam now has to perform both (i) an act such that if he performed it, the shooting of Lincoln would constitute part of the actual past, and (ii) an act such that if he performed it, the shooting of Lincoln would not form part of the actual past.

If the gambit is applicable and we accept the fixity of the past, Sam has the ability of (b) but not the ability of (a). Though distinct, the two abilities are related: (b) is weaker than (a) in the sense that if Sam were to have the ability of (a), he would eo ipso have the ability of (b), but not conversely. It thus seems most plausible to claim that if the ability of (a) satisfies a necessary condition of justified moral responsibility, then so does that of (b). Moreover, we can regard (b)'s satisfaction of a necessary condition for moral responsibility as conforming with the " 'ought' implies 'can' " principle. Although Sam cannot perform the act for which he is to be held morally accountable, he *can* perform some act that results in the act he is being held responsible for. Furthermore, we insist that this ability, this freedom, is necessary if Sam is to be justifiably held accountable. That is to say, if Sam could not perform the act mentioned in (b), then, in accordance with the " 'ought' implies 'can' " principle, it is illegitimate to hold him morally responsible for shooting Lincoln. This shows that the gambit's moral applicability does trivialize the notion of justified attribution of moral responsibility.

It is true that this defense of the gambit's moral applicability coerces an extension of the typical way " 'ought' implies 'can' " is understood. Normally we assume that the selfsame act is the object of the agent's ability as well as being what the agent is held morally responsible for. This defense requires distinct actions to play these roles. Nonetheless, the spirit behind the principle appears to be left intact, and so I believe it is fair to say that this defense is in conformity with a moral principle we would be hesitant to relinquish.

There are other directions from which the Lewis gambit's moral applicability can be questioned. We may focus on an epistemic criterion for moral responsibility.

One might argue that a necessary condition for justified ascription of moral responsibility is that the individual have, or at least possess the ability to have, certain beliefs concerning the outcome of his acts. He must, for example, be able to realize that if he performed a particular act, a person would feel pain, suffer, or be depressed. Although it would be too restrictive to require of warranted moral liability that cognizance of these facts would determine an agent's behavior, it is arguable that the individual, to be considered a moral agent, must at least be able to consider these outcomes as part of his moral calculus. That is, one could argue that a necessary condition for justifiably ascribing moral responsibility is that the agent be capable of being aware of and assessing, in some minimally rough and ready way, the consequences of his action. We often exculpate infants and senile persons because they fail to meet something like this condition. It is quite natural to attempt to mitigate, if not eliminate, responsibility by claiming that an individual was incapable of 'knowing what he was doing' or judging the effects his act could have.

The argument against the Lewis gambit's viability for permitting moral accountability of the past seizes upon this condition, but it situates the inaccessibility of the act's consequences *not* within the agent (as in the case of the infant or senile person) but in the temporal relation that obtains between the agent's action and its consequences. That is, it is not due to some physical or mental disability that such ignorance is guaranteed; rather, the temporal remoteness of the event for which the agent is being held accountable denies him access to the effects of his current actions. The change, then, is that an epistemic condition necessary for legitimate attribution of moral responsibility can be violated by applying the gambit, and thus the gambit's foray into ethics must be abandoned.

The argument claims that an individual could never have any justified beliefs about how the past would be differently constituted were he to perform one of several possible actions. Although it is possible, and indeed frequently simple, to have good reason for thinking one's present actions will have a particular effect on the constitution of the future, the situation is just the reverse when we consider how the past might be constituted.

Let us, arguendo, accept the epistemic principle as a necessary condition of moral responsibility. The question then turns on whether we need accept the argument's suggestion that we are necessarily ignorant about how the past's constitutional differences may vary with the enactment of alternative present actions. It seems that we need not—that in principle our beliefs about how the past may be so constituted are as warranted as our correlative beliefs about the future. Given the truth of determinism, we can just as well infer what had to be the case from what is as we can reason from what is to what will be the case. Retrodiction should be no less certain than prediction. Given the truth of indeterminism, our beliefs about what constituted the past are less certain, but by the same token so are our beliefs concerning the constitution of the future. And even under the aegis of indeterminism, not all possible constitutions of tense need be equiprobable. We may have good reason, albeit not conclusive reason, for believing that the past (or future) will consist of certain events rather than others if in fact we currently perform a particular act.

Another tactic for arguing against the viability of morally applying the Lewis gambit may center on the notion of deliberation. In general form the argument would run as follows: (1) There can be no (full-bodied or meaningful) deliberation concerning the past; (2) the possibility of deliberating about one's actions is required for warranted attribution of moral responsibility; (3) so there cannot be any legitimate moral ascription to agents concerning the past; (4) so any principle that allows for the possibility of such legitimate attribution—as the gambit putatively does—demands rejection.

I want to focus on the first premise, which admittedly appears uninviting from the standpoint of one trying to defend the intelligibility of holding persons responsible for past events. The reasoning for this premise progresses along the following lines: the object or content of our deliberations is courses of action; that is, when we deliberate, we deliberate about what we are going to do. In deliberating, we must believe (or at least assume) that the courses of action under review are real possibilities to us; that is, we must believe we can perform the actions we are deliberating about. This is to be understood not as a psychological claim, but rather as a statement about the logical character of deliberation. It serves as a partial analysis of the concept of "deliberation" or, equivalently, gives us part of the meaning of the term. About past events we can do nothing; that is, we cannot now either modify or undo a past event or bring about a past event. Even if we mistakenly believe we can perform actions that will influence the past's constitution and thus satisfy a necessary condition for deliberation (we might be mistaken about the tense of an event), such deliberation would be pointless—in the sense that, regardless of our decision based on the deliberation, the outcome would be the same.[3] Thus, deliberation concerning an action that is to influence the past either is impossible or is pointless and a sham. In either case, full-bodied deliberation about such a course of action cannot occur.

Despite both the plausibility and popularity of such a line of thought, I believe it ought to be rejected. This rejection is based on the realization that such reasoning proves too much. As an introduction, consider a case that seems to confirm this mode of argument. It seems correct to claim that we cannot deliberate (again, in any meaningful or full-bodied way) about making it rain or not rain. Regardless of the "decision" we reach, it will either rain or not rain, and so such a mental process is pointless and a mere ceremony.

But now consider two other cases, both employing the 'if pointless, then not (real) deliberation' logic. First recall the plight of many mathematicians who at least seemed to deliberate about whether one could trisect an angle using only a compass and straightedge. Regardless of the "decision" they reached, such a trisection would prove impossible, and so the "deliberation" was, according to the principle at hand, a sham. My intuitions, at least, are that we may drop the quoted contexts and talk about meaningful or full-bodied decisions and deliberations. The second example applies to a future event that is not logically mandated. Suppose Jones takes himself to be deliberating about whether to shoot Smith with his gun. Unknown to Jones during this internal debate, the gun is not loaded, and so, regardless of his "decision," Jones will not shoot Smith. Once again, it seems most natural to countenance this as an actual deliberation process culminating in a real decision. (It is quite a different question to ask whether Jones can deliberate about *trying* to use his gun to shoot Smith. Here, I take it, all parties would agree in the affirmative.)

Moreover, even if no deliberation about a past action is (logically) permitted, it is quite a different matter whether deliberation concerning a future event that will eventuate in a certain constitution of the past is also precluded. Thus, even if we allow that in no full-bodied way can Sam deliberate about shooting Lincoln, it requires additional argument to demonstrate that Sam is equally unable to deliberate about a future action of his such that, were it performed, Lincoln's shooting would be a part of the actual past. The onus reverts to those who believe such an additional argument can be supplied.

Let us entertain one final strategy. Perhaps one can plausibly argue that justified ascription of moral responsibility requires, in a broad way, implementing a causal relation between an individual and the act he is held morally accountable for. For this claim to have its putative plausibility, the qualification "in a broad way" must be taken very seriously. This qualification is significant in at least two types of cases. Consider the case of a man hiring someone else to murder somebody. Our intuition—intuition manifested in our courts of law—makes the man who hires at least partially morally responsible for the victim's death. Whether his accountability is less than, equal to, or more than that of the person who pulled the trigger—the man we might naturally say was the "direct cause" of the victim's death—is not at issue here. All that is needed is consensus that the man who offers the money, the "indirect cause" of the victim's death, maintains at least some moral responsibility for it. A second sort of case in which the qualifier comes into play is when we have omissions of acts. Consider the time-honored example of a woman who sits idly by as her young son drowns in the bathtub. Surely, once again, our moral intuition dictates the accountability of the mother, and once again we need not worry about comparing her moral accountability with that of the mother who actually pushes her son's head under the water. Here, though the issues are complicated, it is natural to say that the lack of aid by the mother, an omission of an action, is part of the cause of her son's death, and thus the mother satisfies a necessary condition of justly being held morally responsible.

Let us, then, at least provisionally hold that some causal relation, broadly understood, needs to obtain to justify attributing moral responsibility. Consider, in this light, the Lewis gambit. Implementing this gambit, as I have repeatedly emphasized, does not involve the sensefulness of the notion of modifying (a causal notion) the past. Furthermore, it is neutral on whether it causes the past to have a constitution it would otherwise have lacked. The relation between the implementation of the gambit and the past's ontology could be retrocausal (forwardly) causal, or even acausal. Such acausality is possible even if we adopt a very weak Humean regularity view of causation. For example, it may be the case that if I freely perform action a_1, the past would contain p_1 (whereas the past would otherwise contain p_2), but such a sequence may not regularly occur. There may not be, then, a covering law, which to Hume is nothing more than a description of universal succession, under which this sequence of events can be subsumed. The ploy now is to say that any account that allows for the possibility of no causal relation between agent and act must be dismissed, because such permissibility is inconsistent with a necessary condition for the justified ascription of moral responsibility.

We could even apply this strategy more globally. It seems reasonable to suppose that, necessarily, moral responsibility requires a causal world. The Lewis gambit allows for worlds where moral responsibility and acausality cohabit. Thus the gambit needs to be rejected. It is worth noting that such a strategy is far more plausible than another urged by some—that justified ascription of moral responsibility requires a deter-ministic world.[4] In a deterministic world, causes necessitate (i.e., if in the actual world A causes B, then in every logically possible world congruent with the actual world up to and including A, B is also included). We need not burden causation with this property. (If one is adamant about necessitation's forming part of the concept of causation, we can play the game of inventing the notion of sh-causation, which is just like causation but lacks its allegedly essential ingredient.) Thus an indeterministic world may well have causes. The notion that moral responsibility requires causal efficacy is weaker than the notion that moral responsibility requires determinism and so is implied by, but does not imply, the latter. It is in this sense that it is more plausible.

Let us once again, for the sake of argument, accept the claim that moral responsibility requires a causal world. What we need to realize is that the Lewis gambit is consistent with this requirement even though it allows for an acausal relation between the performed act and the event that forms part of the past's constitution. The causality that is required holds between the agent's free decision to perform a particular (future) action and the occurrence of that action. That is, an advocate of the gambit's moral applicability may hold an old-fashioned volitional view of actions where, roughly, the agent's exercise of his free will causes an action. Other, more complicated accounts may also be held, the only restriction being that such accounts be causal in nature. So the gambit's world is one which causality holds between some sort of events while (perhaps) not holding between other types. Once we are armed with this distinction, the threat to the gambit's moral applicability is again de-terred.

The provisional conclusion, surprising as it may be, is that there is no definitive reason to reject the possibility of moral responsibility toward past events. Since metaphysical fatalism attributes past necessity to all events, we have no decisive suggestions for finding justified ascriptions of moral responsibility incompatible with it. This, to me at least, pro-vides yet another incentive for understanding traditional fatalism as having a metaphysical rather than a logical nature, for it provides us with a far richer arena of inquiry. I realize that an opposite verdict is likely to be voiced; that the relation between moral responsibility and the past that is allowed by metaphysical fatalism serves as a reductio of this rendering of fatalism and that since logical fatalism at least does not permit this absurdity, we have an excellent reason for rejecting the metaphysical interpretation. As with so many issues in philosophy, we reach a stage where one person's *modus ponens* is another's *modus tollens*, and I must here leave readers to adopt the inference form they find most revealing and rewarding.

FIVE

WITTGENSTEINIAN FATALISM

5.1 This chapter, admittedly a highly interpretive exercise concerning Wittgenstein's contribution to the arena of fatalism, will have a somewhat different character and tone than the preceding chapters. Detailed argument will take a subsidiary role to exegesis of a panoramic vision. Visions are not theories, and so even my exegesis, along with some limited commentary, should be viewed as merely an introduction to work that may prove productive. The later Wittgenstein wrote comparatively little about freedom of the will. Perhaps the most sustained picture of his later views can be culled from notes of Yorick Smythies ("Wittgenstein's Notes on the Freedom of the Will," Nachlass, volume 99, Cornell edition, to which all page numbers refer), who attended a lecture Wittgenstein gave in Cambridge sometime in 1945 or 1946. Any interpretation contains some speculation, but the following contains more than most. Since there is virtually no explicit supporting material either from Wittgenstein himself or from commentators, I have relied solely on the methodological constraint that any interpretation of the notes must cohere with what I take, at least, to be the spirit of Wittgenstein's later writings. In certain parts of my exposition (and my aim is exposition, not criticism), I explicitly refer to some points of contact between the Notes and the *Investigations*.

In the Notes, there is no indication that Wittgenstein attempted to distinguish between determinism and fatalism. His concerns, as we shall see, did not require such a distinction. (Many of the ancients also did not distinguish these two theses. Again, this hardly shows confusion or lack of sophistication, as some authors believe; rather, it shows that some of the purposes of the debate have changed in the intervening years.) Nonetheless, many of the comments are easily accommodated by both theses, and it should be evident that many of the insights directed toward determinism are transportable to fatalism. Wittgenstein does not use the term "determinism" univocally. Sometimes it is presented as incompatible with freedom and moral responsibility (in effect being identified with traditional "hard" determinism), while at other times the thesis is conceived as neutral concerning the issues of freedom and moral responsibility. Context serves to disambiguate Wittgenstein's meaning, and so I have followed his usage of the unmodified "determinism" throughout. Moreover, it is evident that Wittgenstein approaches the problem of free will from essentially an ethical perspective. It is from concerns embodying praise and blame that the problem gets its life and significance. There is no clearer indication of this than Wittgenstein's central use of the term "compatibilism," by which he means the thesis that espouses the consistency of determinism and moral responsibility. Furthermore, we should understand Wittgenstein as working within the received view that freedom is necessary for moral responsibility, although I have, in a previous chapter, given some reason to believe that this relationship is more contentious than was commonly thought.

One might ask the justification for including a chapter dealing exclusively with Wittgenstein's thoughts on the matter of free will. One part of my justification is that it is valuable to try to understand what any great mind has to say about any perennial philosophical problem. The other part, far more important, is that on my rendition of the Notes, Wittgenstein has many imaginative, novel, and provocative insights to share. Airing his views can only deepen our understanding of the problem.

5.2 "All these arguments might look as if I wanted to argue for the freedom of the will or against it. But I don't want to" (p. 13). There do appear to be many varied arguments in Wittgenstein's remarks. There seems to be general argumentation to support *some* sort of compatibilism, in the sense that we may be justifiably held morally responsible even though our actions are determined. I suggest that we take Wittgenstein's metaphilosophical remark quite seriously, however. In general, then, I wish to construe Wittgenstein's remarks as offering an alternative picture where, given some obvious facts, we need not view ourselves as mere puppets even if determinism is true. The "fly bottle" he is showing us out of is created by our own fixation of the problem in a certain manner, a manner that neither reason nor logic dictates. We can grasp another picture, a prephilosophical picture, if our attention is not focused in a different direction. Within this framework, we do not view compatibilism and determinism as competing doctrines that try to tell the truth about the way the world really is. Rather, they are just two of the ways of viewing the world, one taking precedence over the other for, usually, psychological reasons. But this does not mean that either view should be taken as merely arbitrary or capricious. It is an important fact concerning the psychology of human beings that we naturally view this issue from a determinist viewpoint once we begin philosophizing. That we do so teaches us about ourselves as well as about the nature of philosophy. "A certain image can force itself upon you" (p. 11). Wittgenstein attempts to demonstrate how we can dispel such an image and allay our doubts about our fundamental ability to ascribe, justifiably, moral responsibility to people.

We should note at the outset just how much Wittgenstein's position differs from that of the (ordinary) compatibilist. The latter can be seen as trying to *justify* our practice of holding people morally responsible even in the face of the truth of determinism. Wittgenstein attempts no such justification; indeed, any attempt to justify or advance arguments in favor of our moral language and moral practices are egregiously misguided. This general chord has been struck several times in the *Investigations*. When Wittgenstein tells us that our spade is turned and that justifications must come to an end, he is warning us that a search for a justification of our fundamental modes of speech and action is doomed to fail. Eventually we reach the point where we can only say "this is what we do." The compatibilist's mistake, then, is that he tries to go too far. By trying to demonstrate a justification of our moral language, the compatibilist sets himself an impossible task, but fortunately it is a task that need never be set. It is in this spirit, I believe, that Wittgenstein wishes to be seen as not forwarding any *arguments* for or against freedom of the will.

Wittgenstein begins with the version of determinism that has it that a statement describing a person's actions can be deduced from statements describing the action's antecedent conditions and natural laws. It is this view of determinism (or something akin to it) that people have in mind when they claim that human actions are compelled—that the "agent" was actually passive (and so there really were no actions performed, but just passions that happened to the person). The person, on this view, has no freedom of choice over what he does. None of his performances are "up to him."

Wittgenstein tries to attack the alleged unavoidability of such a picture from various angles. He first questions the meaningfulness of saying that natural laws are, in fact, compelling. The word "law" already implies the notion of necessity or compulsion and so presupposes the position we are supposed to, ultimately, adopt. It seems, then, that we must begin with a more neutral term, say, "general descriptions of observed regularities." For why do we claim we have discovered a law of nature? We have, for example, seen many stones fall. Eventually we see that the force, mass, and acceleration (say) of the stone can be described by the formula $f = ma$. This formula has described all previous stone fallings (say), and we predict that all future stone fallings will be in accord with this natural law. *Will be,* yes, but why should we say *must be,* as those who claim the stone's behavior is compelled would have us do? What would it mean to say that the stone is compelled to act in such a way by the natural law?

Consider a case where we do say an action is compelled—for example, a train that runs on railroad tracks. Given our background presuppositions, that train tracks do not normally change their shape and trains do not normally skip over tracks, and our knowledge that the tracks are laid out in a determinate manner, we can talk of the tracks' compelling the train to run in a particular direction. But this is only because we can determine the path of the tracks *independent* of the train's movement. For, certainly, from the mere fact that the train always travels on tracks, we could not justifiably speak of the train's being compelled to move in such a manner. Perhaps the train travels randomly, but tracks always appear under it regardless of the direction the train takes. Rather, we apply the notion of compulsion to such a case because, in addition to our sundry knowledge of trains and tracks, we can tell the path of the tracks while disregarding the motion of the train.

The question to ask ourselves now is whether the natural law in the case of a falling stone plays the same role as do the railroad tracks in the case of the moving train. It appears as though, in the former case, the natural law would have to be seen as describing the compelling force of gravity. Gravity, then, compels the stone to behave in accordance with $f = ma$, just as the railroad tracks compel the train to move in a particular direction.

It is evident that Wittgenstein views the railroad tracks and gravity as essentially different. Perhaps this difference can be brought out by noticing the way Wittgenstein apparently conceives of gravity as being introduced into our ontology. Evidently Wittgenstein takes gravity as being the force that moves stones (say) in the direction that falling stones go (whatever that direction may turn out to be). But looked at this way, the notion of gravity as a compelling force seems superfluous, for to say that gravity compels the stone to move in a certain direction is to say no more than that the stone goes as it goes. Conceiving of gravity in this antirealist vein, it is *too* intimately connected with the movement of falling stones to be considered a compelling force.

Notice how this differs from the train/track example. To say that the track compels the motion of the train is not a claim based merely on observed regularities; it is true that some knowledge of the stability of track paths and of train paths on tracks must be presupposed for us to claim compulsion via induction from many instances of trains running on tracks in such and such a manner. (Indeed, I believe Wittgenstein

131

would say we could justifiably claim that 'A compels B', observing just one instance.)

This point can be put slightly differently. That the force of gravity (as Wittgenstein conceives it) works in a particular way can be known only a priori. Thus there is a sense in which we can see the compulsion of the tracks on the train whereas we cannot see the compulsion of gravity on stones. Gravity as a compelling force cannot be distinguished from the motion of falling stones.

Let us now concede that we can speak of natural laws as compelling (governing) stones' movements. But let us ask ourselves why we say the stone is governed by natural laws. Probably because the stone has always moved thus in circumstances C, and we are certain that in future circumstances C the stone will move that way. But can we say this of Jones's or Smith's actions? It is a matter of empirical fact that in what are apparently similar circumstances, Jones will act differently on different occasions. To then counter that *something* (but who knows what) must have been relevantly dissimilar in the two circumstances is to reduce the determinist position to an uninteresting tautology. We simply do not observe the regularity in human behavior that we do in stones' behavior. Perhaps in scores of years, far from finding natural laws that govern human behavior, we will simply give up looking and treat human behavior more or less on the model of electron movement as character- ized by Heisenbergian physics. To say that the stone *does things* and the human being *does things*, and then to infer from this that there is merely a difference in degree in what they do is to stretch any analogy beyond its usefulness. It is even less plausible than saying that because black and white are both colors, there is only a difference of degree between them.

Note that the comparison of the human being with the stone is not the only one we can make. Wittgenstein compares the movement of a steering wheel of a car with human actions. Consider a motor car that follows an irregular path on a level road. We know that the movement of the car is determined by the front wheels (say), which in turn are determined by the steering wheel. The movement of the steering wheel is, as far as we can determine, not determined by anything else. That is, as best we can tell, it moves freely. In the cases of both the steering wheel and the human being we *can* credit freedom to the movements, or we can go on searching for some regularity with the goal of establishing some natural law. It would be mere dogma, however, to claim that there *must* be one natural law that describes the movements of either the steering wheel or the person.

Wittgenstein does believe, though, that an analogy between a stone and a human being may be quite appropriate. Imagine a person in a morose state. He believes that life is "passing him by." He might say something like, "I am like a stone. I have no power over what happens to me. Everything I do turns out badly." Wittgenstein emphasizes that it is important to be aware of the person's past and present circumstances, and even his future actions, in order to know what these words mean when he utters them. In the example offered, we can perhaps take such a person as *expressing* despair and hopelessness. We can empathize with him, and indeed, eliciting sympathy might have been a point of the utterance. The person is not using the sentence to make some sort of scientific statement that may be confirmed or disconfirmed by later developments in science. A search into the sentence's truth-value would be misguided. This account, Wittgenstein apparently believes, can be given to many "free will" statements—for example, statements that are used to express one's taking on or dismissing responsibility.

The importance of this novel "analysis" of such statements cannot be exaggerated. For if it is correct for at least many of the "free will" statements we employ, it would imply that the entire mode of argument used by the determinist is wrong-headed. Wittgenstein believes it would not be quite right to say that scientific advances can have *no* effect on these types of utterances; it is that scientific progress would not have the kind of effect that the determinist needs to further his case. Scientific advances may alter our direction of interest concerning such statements (and so we might, for example, be less likely to utter them), but science will not show that when we did use this type of statement, we said anything false.

The determinist's challenge is often put in terms of predictability of actions. Let me quote Wittgenstein's interlocutor: "Suppose you say: If we really assume that his actions follow natural laws, let us assume that we know these laws; knew the whole working of his cells acting on one another and were therefore able to calculate what he was going to do. This should determine us into saying 'Now we see after all that he isn't responsible for his actions. Ought we to punish him? etc.'" (p. 13). Wittgenstein here grants, for the sake of argument, that we have the possession of natural laws the determinist desires. This knowledge, says the determinist, with the concomitant growth of knowledge in biology and physiology, will allow us to calculate what actions a particular person will perform. This *seems* to preclude freedom of the will, for if we can tell in advance (and, say, in the minutest detail) what action a person will perform, then he could not perform any action other than the one that, in fact, he does perform. So goes the determinist train of thought.

Wittgenstein believes that in such an eventuality we are not logically committed to abstain from ascribing moral responsibility to an individual. He does this in a typical way. He shows us the source of our mental cramp and a method for loosening this cramp. And this is all done by way of an analogy, which, though it is not much more than hinted at, can be filled out, I think, to articulate his point.

Wittgenstein compares the determinist position quoted above to the kidney advertisement, "There are fifteen miles of kidney to clean." This mode of speaking about the kidneys naturally—automatically, as it were—gives one the impression that cleaning the kidneys is a very difficult job. But this task may not be difficult at all. Wittgenstein wishes to make a similar point concerning the alleged inappropriateness of ascribing moral responsibility to a person whose actions can be predicted.

Why do we automatically, even spontaneously, take cleaning fifteen miles of kidneys to be a difficult task? I think it is because we have a certain paradigm (or model, or exemplar) that we implicitly compare the kidney case to—perhaps something like a charwoman cleaning corridors. But this model is inappropriate when we consider the difficulty the circulatory system has in cleaning fifteen miles of kidneys. The body, or circulatory system, does (or we do) the job "effortlessly." There is no intrinsic difficulty in cleaning something that is fifteen miles long, though we are apt to think so because of a certain picture that is (psychologically) persuasive. And escape from this picture may be psychologically impossible. We might not be able to see how the body's cleaning the kidneys can possibly be an easy chore, because we may be unable to rid ourselves of the charwoman paradigm (or something akin to it).

If we were to try to help someone understand how cleaning fifteen miles of kidneys may be easy, we might offer other paradigms that exemplify the ease of cleaning long distances. An example would be a river cleaning its banks. The river has no difficulty cleaning hundreds, even thousands, of miles of its banks. This example may help our friend see that fifteen miles of cleaning is not intrinsically difficult. Or it may not. He still might not be able to see that he is not logically coerced into looking at fifteen miles of cleaning as difficult. Just as a person may be unable to see how the figure ⬜ can represent a (three-dimensional) cube (How can it? It has only two dimensions), in which case the person may be said to suffer from aspect or paradigm blindness, so too he may have the psychological malady of being unable to see fifteen miles of cleaning as a simple task. He might be incapable of seeing fifteen miles of cleaning as a simple task, and he might be incapable of seeing the intended use of our paradigm.

The undertaking now is to show how this "kidney" discussion serves as an analogue to human freedom. First, when we say that the calculation of a person's actions takes place, and that therefore the person cannot be morally responsible, we are in effect treating that person as a machine. That is, we are already using a particular model by which we can understand the predictability of a person's actions as entailing the inappropriateness of ascribing moral responsibility to him. This corresponds to our using the charwoman cleaning corridors as our model for the body cleaning its kidneys. But just as in the kidney case, where we realize that this paradigm does not serve well, we should now be aware that the machine model may not serve us well. Just as cleaning the kidneys may be an easy chore, so too the human body may be held morally responsible. Just as it is true that there are fifteen miles of paths to be cleaned by both the charwoman and the body, and yet the cleaning is not difficult in the latter case, so too it may be true that the actions of a machine and a human being may be predicted, and yet this fact alone may not settle whether moral responsibility is appropriate in the latter case.

Up to this point, the two cases seem to mirror each other well. And one might be satisfied if the discussion ended here. If one realized, or accepted, the claim that fifteen miles of kidneys are easy to clean *without* the aid of an appropriate paradigm, then one should feel comfortable with the analogy up to now. But one may not feel content until and unless one is given a particular paradigm by which we can model a human being who has a moral responsibility. Just as in the kidney case a paradigm was supplied for viewing the cleaning of fifteen miles of paths as easy, so, it seems, one can demand a paradigm for a being whose actions are predictable and yet who is conceived as morally responsible. In short, then, the question is this: What analogue to the river, as used in the example above, can be supplied in the case of the human being?

I believe we have no such paradigm. We do not have an entity that can model the morally responsible human being. And this is why it may be so difficult to rid ourselves of the moral cramp that many of us suffer—viewing a person as some sort of elaborate machine. But rather than despair at this prospect, perhaps we can learn something by it. Our inability to provide such a paradigm shows, I believe, how central the notion of a morally responsible human being is to our conceptual scheme, to the way we think of human beings. We must remember that before we began to philosophize about this subject there was no doubt (in the sense that the question never arose) that human beings were, generally, morally responsible for their actions. Part and parcel of being a normal human being is to be morally accountable. We normally (prephilosophically) have a comparatively small stock of excusing conditions to absolve people of responsibility. We naturally treat human beings as being diametrically opposed to machines, as far as questions of praise, blame, and excuse are concerned. It is only after philosophical inquiry that we begin to question the legitimacy of our moral treatment of persons. It is only when we philosophize that we are drawn to certain analogies that seem to force us into paradoxical and painful conclusions.

Wittgenstein has tried to show us that we are not logically coerced into abandoning our prephilosophical notions. We can thus summarize Wittgenstein's position to this point by saying that predicting an action does not logically exclude free choice. And with free choice goes moral responsibility.

At least concerning some sorts of predictions, this is something we believed all along. If we know a professor's character well, we may be able to predict whether, on a borderline case, he will give a particular student an A rather than a B. In such a case we do not, it seems to me, have an inclination to claim that the professor had no freedom of will or that he simply could not have done otherwise. The situation seems to become much more muddled when the source of the prediction is physical. When the basis of predicting a person's actions is his blood cells and neurons rather than his character traits, prediction is seen as a greater threat to the person's freedom. It is when these types of predictions are made, says the determinist, that we can see most clearly that the human being is just a conglomeration of fancy nuts and bolts. Thus the human being is merely a sophisticated machine and so is equally exempt from moral responsibility.

But from the unerring accuracy of such material predictions we are still not logically coerced into admitting that we lack freedom of the will. We are still not committed to portraying our actions as compelled, because all our observations and predictions are consistent with our prephilosophical view that it is we, the persons, who are the cause of our actions. It is quite consonant with the data that the determinist cites to claim that we freely perform actions, although when we do so our bodies are in a certain predictable state. To rule out the possibility of freedom of the will, the determinist would have to base his predictions on more than the mere observation that a body's being in state S is always followed by action A; he would also be required to observe that S is the *cause* of A.

It is at this juncture that one must exercise extreme caution lest an egregious misunderstanding of Wittgenstein take place. Wittgenstein is *not,* as one might think at first blush, endorsing a Humean skepticism concerning the notion of causation. He is not claiming, as some philosophers think Hume did, that there really is no process of causation occurring in the external world. Concerning this discussion, at least, there is no question that on certain occasions we do see the 'because'. These cases are most clearly exemplified by our normal cases of compelled action. Cases such as one man's pushing another man, or train tracks' governing a train's motion would be examples.

We should also be careful not to construe 'observe' in the 'observing (seeing) the because' as applying only to physical phenomena such as people and train tracks. We can legitimately speak of observing a hypnotic suggestion or a state of drunkenness as causing some action. Nor should it be thought that hypnotic suggestions and the like are not, somehow, as real a cause of an action as one person's shoving another. It is not even true that shoves are easier to verify as causes than are hypnotic suggestions. It may in fact be quite difficult to discern whether a shove was the cause of a man's movement (perhaps he slipped) and relatively easy to identify a hypnotic suggestion as the cause of a man's action. It is interesting that on most occasions when we single out the cause of one's action as a hypnotic suggestion or a state of drunkenness, the action performed will be "out of character." Imagine that Jones habitually yells and screams at his neighbor. If he had imbibed excessively several hours before his usual argument, we would be unlikely to cite his drunkenness as the cause of his arguing. If Smith, who virtually never raises his voice, got drunk shortly before he began shouting at his neighbor, we might very well credit his drunkenness with causing his unseemly behavior. He might very well say that his drunkenness compelled his behavior; his behavior would thus be excusable. None of this proves that our "in character" actions are not compelled (to believe that it does would amount to espousing a paradigm case argument), but it does, I think, point out how unnatural and extreme the determinist's position really is.

This brings us to the final discussion in the Notes. The determinist claims that our *choices*, as well as our actions, are determined by natural laws and that therefore we can never choose other than what we do in fact choose.

There certainly are cases where we say that the person could not have chosen otherwise than he did. These cases are fairly rare. An example might be a person who, under hypnosis, was given a suggestion that he is to choose a certain way when he awakes. Or perhaps it would be correct to say that after excessive imbibing a person could not have chosen otherwise—that his choice was not up to him (and so was not really a choice at all). The determinist assimilates all cases of apparent choice to these pseudochoices. We are always in the same metaphysical position as the hypnotized person or the drunk.

Prima facie, this is an odd assimilation. We ordinarily distinguish between these types of cases. Although there may be difficult epistemological problems in ascertaining *if* the hypnotism or drunkenness really did cause what was apparently no loss of self-control, once we do so our moral judgments are affected accordingly.

Let us give ourselves a concrete case and ask the criterion for its being true to say, in this case, that the person could have chosen otherwise than he in fact did. That is, first let us see what we do, how we act. Then we must ask ourselves if the determinist's claim coerces us to say that we never freely perform actions.

Before me lie a pen and a pencil. I choose to pick up the pen, and I do so. What is the criterion for the apparent truth of the claim that I could have chosen to pick up the pencil? Well, suppose I then set down the pen, choose to pick up the pencil, and do so. Is this enough to show that on the first occasion it would have been true to say that I could have chosen to pick up the pencil? Surely this would be sufficient in non-philosophical circumstances. This is where expressions such as 'could have done (chosen) otherwise' have their home, and we should be wary of any attempt to tell us this thought experiment has no bearing at all on the question.

What is it that we are certain has changed in the circumstances from the first to second case? Time has passed. But it seems difficult to understand how the mere passage of time can be efficacious. Second, what I chose to do has changed. But surely this is not to be counted as part of the antecedent conditions in either of the two cases. That is, the determinist cannot argue that my choosing differently on the two occasions is the difference in the two cases and so the two occasions are relevantly dissimilar. Rather, that I chose to do a particular action is a result of antecedent conditions that, ex hypothesi, differ only in temporal sequence. To say that this assumption cannot be true, that since I chose different courses of action there *must* have been some relevant difference in the antecedent conditions, is to make a remark on faith—one that we are supposing is not supported by empirical evidence.

Compare this case with one where I am hypnotized and told to "choose" to pick up the pencil. Here all parties would agree that I could not have done otherwise, that the choice was not "up to me." We feel this way *not* because we can predict what the individual will do (although, in fact, we can), but rather because we know that some strange manipulations have been going on with the subject's mind. This seems to be the deciding issue not only for the epistemic point of knowing when someone performs an action unfreely, but for the metaphysical status of the act as well. Predictability, then, is irrelevant to the question of freedom.

On the face of it, the assimilation the determinist espouses is quite odd. He wants us to view the truth of determinism as akin to a hypnotic suggestion. He claims that once we realize that our choices as well as our actions can be predicted with complete accuracy, we will realize that our belief in freedom of the will is mere illusion. Our choices are no more up to us than when we are placed under hypnosis. Ignorance of this compulsion is unwarranted bliss.

I have tried to fight the inexorability of such a picture in a Wittgensteinian way, but the determinist may make a last attempt to show that his picture of the world is the (only) correct one. It is on this attempt that Wittgenstein's remarks are focused.

Consider a person P who can predict what another person C will choose to do. So complete are P's predictive powers that he can even predict the process of choosing that C will go through. Suppose P tells C what P predicted. We would then see, says Wittgenstein's interlocutor, that this "choice" and its preceding process were mere shams. There really was no choice or process of choice (deliberation) that took place, since what C was to choose, as well as the process that entered his choice, was already known by C. The intuitive idea, then, is this: How can a person truly go through a process of choosing, of deliberation (a process that seems to necessitate a state of ignorance on the chooser's part), while he all the time *knows* what the road of his deliberation will be as well as its result? We seem to demand contradictory states of mind of such an individual—knowledge and ignorance. The conclusion the interlocutor draws from such a case is that both such a process of choosing and the choice itself are shams.

Wittgenstein believes there is a way out. Rather than viewing this situation as one in which the discovery of such natural laws showed us that we never, even in times of ignorance of such laws, had any freedom of the will, we can view the discovery of such laws as "changing the business" of free will, making it the case that *now* we do not have freedom of the will, in the sense that a person does not deliberate when he has knowledge of a true prediction. But this should not be seen as saying that one has lost a particular power; rather, in situations where one is told a prediction and believes what one is told, there simply is no power to exercise. It is not that the new knowledge one has gained has removed something one would otherwise have; rather, the acquisition of this knowledge makes it a situation where the question of choice no longer arises. It is in this sense that Wittgenstein says that this new knowledge would "change the business" of free will.

Consider the case of M, who is deciding whether to give a borderline student an A or a B. An intimate friend (N) of M who is watching his friend agonize over his decision tells M that he will give the student an A. This prediction of M's friend is based on his long acquaintance with M's character (although it would make no difference to the case were the source of the prediction M's neurons and blood cells).

Upon hearing his friend's prediction, M immediately believes him, realizing that N knows his character well. It is tempting at this point to say that, given that M knows what he is going to do, M cannot choose. But I believe this is a bit misleading. It gives the impression that M, try as he might to choose a course of action, is frustrated by his newly accumulated knowledge. The point is that with this new knowledge, there is nothing to choose; the process of choosing loses its point. Compare this with the case of a man who goes to work every day because he knows this is the only way to support his family. On a nondescript Tuesday morning he wakes up, knowing full well that he will be going to work. The question of choosing to go to work never occurs to him. He *does* not choose. It is not that having knowledge of p and choosing to do p are logically incompatible; it is that having knowledge of p and choosing to do p do not fit.

At any rate, this discovery of natural laws would have no effect on the claim that we have free will *before* the discovery. This is similar to the case where one truly does deliberate when one does not have knowledge, in advance, of a true prediction. So it is not as though our current apprehension of our free will is illusory, any more than it is true that the great majority of our present deliberations are shams. (The interlocutor could hold that all our deliberations are shams, but the statement is made in a context where there is agreement that a distinction can be made between authentic and sham deliberations.) Yet Wittgenstein makes an even stronger and more controversial point. Even if such a prediction were possible and we had knowledge of it, choosing would not automatically become illusory; our apprehension of our own free will would not, ipso facto, be deceptive. We could still say we had a choice, only the point of choosing had become different. And though some might be tempted to say that once the point of choosing has changed we have some phenomenon other than choosing, we are not logically committed to such a position.

Consider the game of roulette, where the two participants know in advance of each spinning of the wheel whether the ball will stop in a red or a black slot. Must the element of "choosing red or choosing black" now be illusory? Must such a choice now be a sham and so not really a choice at all? Wittgenstein answers no; although the point of the game has surely changed (it *would* be a sham to now consider the point of choosing to be a guess as to which colored slot the ball will fall into), we can still play the very same game (roulette) and participate in the same activity (choosing). Roulette now may be played for aesthetic enjoyment. I know very well, for example, that the sun will rise every morning, and in the same general area of the sky, and yet I still can get great pleasure from watching the sunrise each morning. The same may be true of my watching a ball land in the slot where I know it will land. And whereas before the point of choosing the color of the slot the ball would land in was to make a prediction and try to win money, it now may be practiced as an activity that gives the chooser pleasure.

One might simply not accept the crucial claim that a change in the point of choosing does not necessitate a change in activity; one might argue that the point plays an essential role in the activity. Wittgenstein has given his antiessentialist views in the *Investigations* in his discussion concerning family resemblances. If one is not convinced by these comments that the essentialist position has a viable alternative, then I suppose this recent discussion will appear unconvincing. But one who does see Wittgenstein's remarks as offering a realistic conception of the use of general terms applying to the world will have no difficulty in seeing that there is no sharp demarcation between a game of roulette (or an activity like choosing) and something that closely approximates it but is not to be correctly characterized as such a game (or activity). This explains Wittgenstein's otherwise cryptic remark, when discussing choosing (and thus implicitly the roulette case), that "you can call it a different game or not call it a different game."

The upshot is this. If prediction was possible, it would change the point of choosing. Whether it would change it enough so that it should no longer be called "choosing" is not a question with a clear-cut answer. Perhaps for some situations it would be best to consider this activity as choosing and for others it would not. But at least this much is clear: Wittgenstein believes we would not be logically coerced into denying the alleged fact that we would still have freedom of the will, simpliciter, even if all our actions could be fully predicted. In this conclusion we find agreement with the kidney analogy. We cannot say now that certain scientific advances will force us to give up our deep belief that we do have freedom of choice, and for this reason, at least, we should feel more optimistic in our prephilosophical reflections about our freedom of the will.[1]

1 By "tenses" I refer to the metaphysical categories of time—the past, present, and future. I do not denote any grammatical or linguistic expressions, although of course such expressions ('was', 'will be', etc.) are frequently used to indicate tense. I make no attempt to justify the existence of tenses; suffice it to say that all but radical McTaggartians and Parmenideans would find such acceptance platitudinous. I say a bit more about this in chapter 2.

2 Although this discussion has been cast in the terminology appropriate to the moving conception of time, it could be stated assuming a "static" conception. (Much more of the significance, or lack thereof, of a tensed and tenseless vocabulary is discussed in chap. 2.)

3 Cf. [53] for a complementary viewpoint. I remain neutral on whether Naylor's particular criticism of D. Lewis is warranted.

CHAPTER TWO

1 RT, as we will see presently, is given by

'p' is true if and only if p.

This is a weak thesis for two reasons. First, no ontological commitments are made for the nature of the propositions mentioned on the left-hand side of the biconditional. Second, and analogously, the nature of the state of affairs is left open. It is completely neutral whether such states of affairs are essentially mental (subjectivism), are a product of social practices and conventions (intersubjectivism), are identifiable with some person-independent reality (objectivism), or have some other character completely. It is a restricted thesis in that it loses plausibility when, for example, the propositions contain indexical terms. Fortunately, in our discussion of fatalism these considerations are not pertinent. All we need accept is that the plausibility of RT is not diminished if the propositions in question are future tensed. Thus " 'snow will be white' is true if and only if snow will be white" is just as plausible as " 'snow is white' is true if and only if snow is white." For our purposes, contra some interpretations of Aristotle, the legitimacy of future-tense claims and their corresponding facts will not be at issue, although *when* a future-tense claim is true and *when* a future fact obtains will prove to be hotly contested issues. Finally, the notion that propositions correspond to states of affairs is Tarskian in spirit. Tarski explicitly expresses the desire that his definition of truth do justice to our ordinary intuitions concerning truth, intuitions that are well expressed in Aristotle's passage quoted earlier (cf. [75], 49). He then adds that "if we wished to adapt ourselves to modern philosophical terminology, we could perhaps express this conception by means of the familiar formula 'the truth of a sentence consists in its agreement with (or correspondence to) reality'." He later adds that "we could possibly use for the same purpose the following phrase 'a sentence is true if it designates an existing state of affairs'." Although he finds none of these formulations sufficiently precise and clear, he believes that Aristotle's jargonless account is the best of the lot.

2 The proof (following [42]) is as follows:

1	$Tp \lor Fp$	PB
2	$Fp \equiv TNp$	assumption concerning relation between truth and falsity
3	$Tp \lor TNp$	Substitution
4	$p \lor Np$	RT

3 In [79], chap. 2, van Inwagen exploits the same idea.

4 Presumably the fatalist views the internal and external temporal predications omnitemporally.

5 The literature on this subject has grown immensely within the past two decades. For a good introduction to the subject see [25]. A. Grunbaum's

"The Status of Temporal Becoming," in [25], 322–54, has become a locus classicus for the view that the movement of time has only subjective reality. And [43], [45], and [77] advocate an "objectivism" concerning temporal flow, while [64] proffers criticism of this view. In [55] there is an excellent overview of the debate. I have assiduously avoided the popular terms "A-theory" and "B-theory," because the commitments of such theories are by no means univocal. Cf. [55] for some of the non-monolithic suppositions of A-theorists and B-theorists.

6 Thus, even on the assumption that an open future requires an objective indeterminacy, this does not necessitate disavowing atemporalism. At most it demands yielding omnitemporalism. McCall [41, 43], by failing to distinguish adequately between atemporalism and omnitemporalism, succumbs to this confusion.

7 This strategy is reflected in Ockhamism, a compatibilist position concerning God's foreknowledge and human freedom. According to Ockhamists, there are some "nongenuine" or relational facts about a time that involve not only that time but some other time as well. In the case at hand, the Ockhamist would claim that the fact deals not only with the time 1000 B.C., but also with A.D. 1995, and so we cannot simply apply our intuitions about the fixity (inviolability) of the past. Typically, not all relational (or "soft") facts are thought to be such that we have the power to bring about their nonoccurrence, and so the debate centers not so much on whether there are "soft" facts as on which "soft" facts are fixed. Cf. [17], [18], and [32].

8 This account of past changing is based on Lewis's formulation of law-breaking. Cf. [39], [19], and [32].

9 A fully convincing argument for these points would vindicate a particular theory of backtracking conditionals. An interesting difference in views can be found in [4] and in [38]. In [44] McCall presents a variant of the theory espoused in [38].

CHAPTER THREE

1 For determinism to have any plausibility whatever, we need to think of the natural laws of the actual world as being, at least fundamentally, nonstatistical. For suppose our laws were statistical. This would entail

that there are logically possible worlds with laws (and pasts) identical to ours that contain future events distinct from those occurring in our world. That is, as I use the term "statistical law," such logical possibilities exist. Thus, if we allowed our laws to be statistical, determinism could be shown a priori false.

2 Cf. [27] and [79]. Also see [68] for an example of someone who casts a suspicious eye on such a maneuver.

3 An exception is Richard Taylor, who apparently does not find such reasoning fallacious. Cf. [76], chap. 6.

4 The contemporary locus classicus is [15].

5 This is neither to dismiss nor to denigrate the recent work of Donnellan, Kripke, and Putnam, who among other significant contributors in the philosophy of language have emphasized the schism between meaning and essence. Conflating these will aid exposition without distorting the issue.

6 The dictionary is *Webster's New World Dictionary of the American Language*, 2d college ed. (New York: World, 1972).

7 It is worth comparing this discussion with Richard Taylor's conclusion in "I Can," *Philosophical Review* 69 (1960): 78–79: " 'I can move my finger' does not mean what it ever means when applied to physical things. . . . And this is, certainly, a philosophically baffling expression which I feel sure no one can ever analyze; yet it is something that is well understood."

8 Cf. [12] as a notable exception.

9 I would be remiss not to mention J. L. Austin's often-quoted and highly appropriate remark ("If and Cans," reprinted in *Free Will and Determinism*, ed. B. Berofsky [New York: Harper and Row, 1966]): "On philosophy it is *can* in particular that we seem so often to uncover, just when we had thought some problem settled, grinning residually up at us like the frog at the bottom of the beer mug."

CHAPTER FOUR

1 Some philosophers, such as Kripke and van Inwagen, have suggested that the transworld identity of persons is a pseudoproblem. Others, such as Lewis, have developed a rather sophisticated ontology to try, among

other things, to resolve the substantive problem they see as existing. For our purposes, we need not become embroiled in such a dispute.

2   Martinich offers much the same rejoinder, but without the theoretical backing I try to supply.

3   It is interesting to note that pointlessness, so understood, does not imply inefficiency. Somewhat more rigorously, 'if deliberation D concerning action Q is pointless' is understood as 'regardless of the decision that culminates D, Q occurs,' then D may still be efficacious, in the straightforward sense that it may be owing to D that Q occurs. This is just what happens in cases of preemptive causation. Van Inwagen, then, in echoing the view of many, is wrong when he says, "And it seems to be a feature of our concept of deliberation that we can deliberate about which of various mutually exclusive courses of action to pursue only if we believe that each of these courses of action is open to us" ([79], 30). But as one might suppose, I would not push this objection very forcefully. How should we resolve our differences about "a feature of our concept of deliberation"? The dictionary does not help; we both know what "deliberation" means. At root, I believe, the dispute is verbal.

4   Probably [31] and [54] are two of the clearest apologies for such a position, but a similar position seems to be held, at least implicitly, by a great many compatibilists. For the opposite viewpoint—that freedom is compatible with indeterminism—cf. [21], and [11], chap. 15.

CHAPTER FIVE

1   I thank Ben Armstrong, Noel Fleming, William Forgie, Hubert Schwyzer, William Smith, and Burleigh Wilkins for helping me better understand the Notes.

BIBLIOGRAPHICAL ESSAY

INTRODUCTION

For historically based book-length treatments of fatalism, one should consult Sorabji, *Necessity, Cause, and Blame*, and White, *Agency and Integrality*. To the best of my knowledge, there has been no problem-oriented approach in the recent past. One way of understanding my thesis is that this gap in the literature is worth filling.

Sorabji is especially helpful for his discussion of Aristotle's sea battle, which I discuss in some detail in chapter 2. White covers wider historical territory and is more exegetical; for a review of his book, see Bernstein, in *Nous* 23 (June 1989): 391–94.

CHAPTER ONE

The contemporary locus classicus of the referential/attributive distinction is Donnellan, "Reference and Definite Descriptions." A major challenge to the drawing of this distinction is Kripke, "Speaker's Reference and Semantic Reference."

For a very recent quite readable work that deals in part with the notion of an open future and a closed past, see Horwich, *Asymmetries in Time*. There is also a rather quick dismissal of fatalism, indicative of the lack of respect many philosophers have shown toward this thesis.

The classic paper contending that there is no analytic/synthetic distinction is Quine, "Two Dogmas of Empiricism." The immediate response is Grice and Strawson, "In Defense of a Dogma."

The modern ancestor of the immense interest in analyses of causal and counterfactual claims is Hume's discussion in section 7 of the *Enquiry concerning Human Understanding*. The key paragraph may be worth noting: "Suitably to this experience, therefore, we may define a cause to be an object, followed by another, and where all objects similar to the first are followed by objects similar to the second. Or in other words where, if the first object had not been, the second never had existed." As one would imagine, responses to how counterfactuals should be treated vary enormously. In Quine, *Methods of Logic*, we are given reasons not to countenance them at all. A more popular view has been "metalinguistic analysis" (Goodman, *Fact, Fiction, and Forecast*; Chisholm, "The Contrary-to-Fact Conditional"; Mackie, "Counterfactuals and Causal Laws"), which claims that a counterfactual is true (or assertable) if and only if its antecedent together with appropriate further premises implies its consequent. For a distinctly different approach, 'similarity analysis,' see Lewis, *Counterfactuals*, and Stalnaker, "A Theory of Conditionals." For one attempt to rejuvenate the older metalinguistic view (which, the author admits, ultimately fails), see Halpin, "Counterfactual Analysis."

CHAPTER TWO

The classic text favoring an ontology of tensed truths is Aristotle's *De interpretatione*, book 9. Modern apologists who further argue for the ineliminability of tensed facts are Gale, in *The Language of Time*, and Prior, in "Changes in Events and Changes in Things." The new breed of tenseless theorists now admit that tenseless paraphrase of all tensed utterances is impossible, but nonetheless they claim that tensed statements do not ascribe tenses (i.e., that no properties of presentness, pastness, or futurity are being imputed). (See Smart, "Time and Becoming"; Mellor, *Real Time*; Oaklander, *Temporal Relations and Temporal Becoming*; and Beer, "Temporal Indexicals and the Passage of Time.") For responses to this new strategy, see Priest, "Tense and Truth Conditions"; Smith, "The Co-repeating Theory of Tensed and Tenseless Sentences"; and Swineburne, "Tensed Facts." See Oaklander, *Temporal Relations and Temporal Becoming* for an extended bibliography and perhaps the clearest, fairest, and most fully articulated account of the debate between tensers and nontensers. In "Fatalism and Time," I try to show how the typical marriage between fatalism and tenseless propositions that is prevalent in the literature is a consequence of a gross misunderstanding.

CHAPTER THREE

For just a short list of philosophers who have believed that retrocausation is impossible, see Tolman, *The Theory of Relativity of Motion*; Flew, "Can an Effect Precede Its Cause?"; Black, "Why Cannot an Effect Precede Its Cause?"; Pears, "The Priority of Causes"; and Mellor, *Real Time*.

The basic strategy employed against the possibility of retrocausation is to allow the reputed (temporally prior) effect to occur and then try to prevent the occurrence of the reputed (temporally subsequent) cause. If this attempt succeeds, causation is said not to hold; if the attempt fails, it is said that the cause and effect have been mislabeled. See Horwich, *Asymmetries in Time* (esp. 91–110), for a response to this line of thought.

The best treatment of paradigm case arguments I know is still Passmore, "Arguments to Meaninglessness." Passmore's critique comes on the heels of the use to which many ordinary-language philosophers (e.g., Moore, Urmson, Flew) put this form of argument.

CHAPTER FOUR

Perhaps the two most significant papers concerning the Principle of Alternate Possibilities are Frankfurt, "Alternate Possibilities and Moral Responsibility," and van Inwagen, "Ability and Responsibility." In the latter, van Inwagen argues that although Frankfurt's attack against PAP is strictly speaking successful, replacement principles can be formulated that capture the spirit of PAP while maintaining immunity from Frankfurt-style counterexamples. Frankfurt offers a reply in "What Are We Morally Responsible For?" In "Responsibility and Control," Fischer argues against some aspects of van Inwagen's attack while attempting to show how one can agree that determinism and responsibility are incompatible and yet hold, with Frankfurt, that responsibility does not require control. In "Moral Responsibility, Freedom, and Alternate Possibilities," Zimmerman argues, in effect, that even if we grant Frankfurt success in his attack against PAP, this does not in itself establish compatibility of moral responsibility and causal determinism.

In "Three Concepts of Free Action: I," Locke argues that Frankfurt's theory is too restrictive concerning the avoidance of moral responsibility. Frankfurt's response to this can be found in "Three Concepts of Free Action: II."

Other papers worthy of review are Strasser, "Frankfurt, Aristotle, and PAP," and Naylor, "Frankfurt on the Principle of Alternate Possibilities." If one is truly desperate one might consult my own contribution, "Moral Responsibility and Free Will."

REFERENCES

[1] Austin, J. L. "Performative Utterances." In *Philosophical Papers*, 2d ed., ed. J. O. Urmson and G. J. Warnock, 233–52. Oxford: Oxford University Press, 1970.

[2] Ayer, A. J. "Fatalism." In *Concept of a Person and Other Essays*, 235–68. London: Macmillan, 1963.

[3] Beer, Michelle. "Temporal Indexicals and the Passage of Time." *Philosophical Quarterly* 30 (April 1988): 158–64.

[4] Bennett, J. "Counterfactuals and Temporal Direction." *Philosophical Review* 93 (January 1984): 57–92.

[5] Bernstein, Mark. "Moral Responsibility and Free Will." *Southern Journal of Philosophy* 19 (1983): 1–10.

[6] Bernstein, Mark. Review of *Agency and Integrality*. *Nous* 23 (June 1989): 391–94.

[7] Bernstein, Mark. "Fatalism and Time." *Dialogue* 28 (1989): 461–71.

[8] Black, Max. "Why Cannot an Effect Precede Its Cause?" *Analyses* 16 (January 1956): 49–58.

[9] Blumenfeld, David. "The Principle of Alternate Possibilities." *Journal of Philosophy* 68 (June 1971): 334–45.

[10] Chisholm, Roderick. "The Contrary-to-Fact Conditional." *Mind* 55 (October 1946): 289–307.

[11] Dennett, Daniel. *Brainstorms: Philosophical Essays on Mind and Psychology*. Cambridge: Bradford Books, 1978.

[12] Dennett, Daniel. *Elbow Room*. Cambridge: MIT Press, 1984.

[13] Donnellan, Keith. "Reference and Definite Descriptions." *Philosophical Review* 75 (July 1966): 281–304.

[14] Driver, Julia. "Promises, Obligations, and Abilities." *Philosophical Studies* 44 (September 1983): 221–24.

[15] Dummett, Michael. "Bringing about the Past." *Philosophical Review* 73 (July 1964): 338–59.

[16] Fischer, J. M. "Responsibility and Control." *Journal of Philosophy* 79 (January 1982): 24–40.

[17] Fischer, J. M. "Freedom and Foreknowledge." *Philosophical Review* 92 (January 1983): 67–79.

[18] Fischer, J. M. "Ockhamism." *Philosophical Review* 94 (January 1985): 80–100.

[19] Fischer, J. M. "Van Inwagen on Free Will." *Philosophical Quarterly* 36 (April 1986): 252–60.

[20] Flew, A. "Can an Effect Precede Its Cause?" *Proceedings of the Aristotelian Society* (suppl.) 38 (1954): 45–62.

[21] Foot, Philippa. "Free Will as Involving Determinism." *Philosophical Review* 66 (October 1957): 439–50.

[22] Frankfurt, Harry. "Alternate Possibilities and Moral Responsibility." *Journal of Philosophy* 66 (December 1969): 828–39.

[23] Frankfurt, Harry. "Three Concepts of Free Action: II." *Proceedings of the Aristotelian Society* (suppl.) 49 (1975): 113–25.

[24] Frankfurt, Harry. "What Are We Morally Responsible For?" In *How Many Questions?* ed. Leigh Cauman et al., 321–35. Indianapolis: Hackett, 1982.

[25] Gale, Richard M., ed. *The Philosophy of Time*. New York: Anchor-Doubleday, 1967.

[26] Gale, Richard M., ed. *The Language of Time*. London: Routledge and Kegan Paul, 1968.

[27] Ginet, Carl. "Might We Have No Free Choice?" In *Freedom and Determinism*, ed. K. Lehrer, 87–104. New York: Random House, 1966.

[28] Goodman, Nelson. *Fact, Fiction, and Forecast*. Cambridge: Harvard University Press, 1954.

[29] Grice, H. P., and P. F. Strawson. "In Defense of a Dogma." *Philosophical Review* 55 (April 1956): 141–58.

[30] Halpin, John. "Counterfactual Analysis: Can the Metalinguistic Theory Be Revitalized?" *Synthese* 81 (October 1989): 47–62.

[31] Hobart, R. E. "Freewill as Involving Determinism." *Mind* 43 (January 1934): 1–28.

[32] Hoffman, J., and G. Rosenkrantz. "Hard and Soft Facts." *Philosophical Review* 93 (July 1984): 414–34.

[33] Horgan, T. "Compatibilism and the Consequence Argument." *Philosophical Studies* 47 (May 1985): 339–56.

[34] Horwich, Paul. *Asymmetries in Time: Problems in the Philosophy of Science.* Cambridge: MIT Press, 1987.

[35] Hume, David. "Of Liberty and Necessity." In *An Enquiry concerning Human Understanding,* 364ff. New York: Anchor Press, 1974.

[36] Kripke, Saul. "Speaker's Reference and Semantic Reference." In *Contemporary Perspectives in the Philosophy of Language,* ed. P. French, T. E. Uehling, Jr., and H. K. Wettstein, 6–27. Minneapolis: University of Minnesota Press, 1977.

[37] Lewis, D. K. *Counterfactuals.* Cambridge: Harvard University Press, 1973.

[38] Lewis, D. K. "Counterfactual Dependence and Time's Arrow." *Nous* 13 (November 1979): 455–76.

[39] Lewis, D. K. "Are We Free to Break the Laws?" *Theoria* 47 (1981): 113–21.

[40] Locke, Don. "Three Concepts of Free Action: I." *Proceedings of the Aristotelian Society* (suppl.) 49 (1975): 95–112.

[41] McCall, S. "Temporal Flux." *American Philosophical Quarterly* 3 (October 1966): 270–81.

[42] McCall, S. "A Non-classical Theory of Truth with an Application to Intuitionism." *American Philosophical Quarterly* 7 (January 1970): 83–88.

[43] McCall, S. "Objective Time Flow." *Philosophy of Science* 43 (September 1976): 337–62.

[44] McCall, S. "Counterfactuals Based on Real Possible Worlds." *Nous* 18 (September 1984): 463–78.

[45] McCall, S. "A Dynamic Model of Temporal Becoming." *Analysis* 44 (October 1984): 172–76.

[46] MacKenzie, J. S. "Eternity." In *The Encyclopedia of Religion and Ethics,* ed. J. Hastings. New York: Scribners, 1912.

[47] Mackie, J. L. "Counterfactuals and Causal Laws." In *Analytical Philosophy*, ed. R. T. Butler, 66–80. Blackwell: Oxford University Press, 1962.

[48] Martinich, A. P. "A Solution to a Paradox of Promising." *Philosophia* 15 (September 1985): 117–22.

[49] Martinich, A. P. "Obligation, Ability, and Prima Facie Promising." *Philosophia* 17 (October 1987): 323–30.

[50] Maugham, Somerset. "Sheppy," act 3. In *The Collected Plays of W. Somerset Maugham*. London, 1931.

[51] Mellor, D. H. *Real Time*. Cambridge: Cambridge University Press, 1981.

[52] Naylor, Margery. "Frankfurt on the Principle of Alternate Possibilities." *Philosophical Studies* 46 (September 1984): 249–58.

[53] Naylor, Margery. "A Note on David Lewis's Realism about Possible Worlds." *Analysis* 46 (January 1986): 28–29.

[54] Nowell-Smith, P. H. "Freewill and Moral Responsibility." *Mind* 57 (January 1948): 45–61.

[55] Oaklander, N. *Temporal Relations and Temporal Becoming: A Defense of a Russellian Theory of Time*. Lanham, Md.: University Press of America, 1984.

[56] Oaklander, N. "A Defense of the New Tenseless Theory of Time." Photocopied, 1988.

[57] Passmore, John. "Arguments to Meaninglessness: Excluded Opposites and Paradigm Cases." In *Philosophical Reasoning*, 100–118. New York: Scribner's, 1961.

[58] Pears, David. "The Priority of Causes." *Analysis* 17 (January 1957): 54–63.

[59] Priest, Graham. "Tense and Truth Conditions." *Analysis* 46 (1986): 162–66.

[60] Prior, A. N. "Thank Goodness That's Over." *Philosophy* 34 (January 1959): 12–17.

[61] Prior, A. N. "Changes in Events and Changes in Things." Lindley Lecture, University of Kansas, 1962.

[62] Quine, W. V. *Methods of Logic*. New York: Holt, Rinehart, and Winston, 1959.

[63] Quine, W. V. "Two Dogmas of Empiricism." In *From a Logical Point of View*, 2d ed., 20–46. Cambridge: Harvard University Press, 1961.

[64] Schlesinger, G. *Aspects of Time.* Indianapolis: Hackett, 1980.

[65] Schlossberger, E. "Why We Are Responsible for Our Emotions." *Mind* 95 (January 1986): 37–56.

[66] Searle, John. "What Is a Speech Act?" In *Philosophy in America*, ed. M. Black, 221–39. Ithaca, N.Y.: Cornell University Press, 1965.

[67] Sinnott-Armstrong, W. "A Resolution to a Paradox of Promising." *Philosophia* 17 (January 1987): 77–82.

[68] Slote, Michael. "Selective Necessity and Free Will." *Journal of Philosophy* 74 (January 1982): 5–24.

[69] Smart, J. J. C. "Time and Becoming." In *Time and Cause*, ed. P. van Inwagen, 3–15. Dordrecht: Reidel, 1980.

[70] Smith, Quentin. "The Co-repeating Theory of Tensed and Tenseless Sentences." *Philosophical Quarterly* 40 (April 1990): 213–21.

[71] Sorabji, Richard. *Necessity, Cause, and Blame: Perspectives on Aristotle's Theory.* Ithaca, N.Y.: Cornell University Press, 1983.

[72] Stalnaker, Robert. "A Theory of Conditionals." *Theoria* 36 (1970): 23–42.

[73] Strasser, Mark. "Frankfurt, Aristotle, and PAP." *Southern Journal of Philosophy* 26 (Summer 1988): 235–46.

[74] Swineburne, Richard. "Tensed Facts." *American Philosophical Quarterly* (April 1990): 117–30.

[75] Tarski, A. "The Semantic Conception of Truth and the Foundations of Semantics." In *Philosophy of Language*, ed. A. P. Martinich, 48–71. Oxford: Oxford University Press, 1985.

[76] Taylor, Richard. *Metaphysics.* 3d ed. Englewood Cliffs, N.J.: Prentice-Hall, 1983.

[77] Tolman, R. C. *The Theory of Relativity of Motion.* Berkeley: University of California Press, 1917.

[78] Van Inwagen, Peter. "Ability and Responsibility." *Philosophical Review* 87 (April 1978): 201–24.

[79] Van Inwagen, Peter. *An Essay on Free Will.* Oxford: Clarendon Press, 1983.

[80] White, Michael. *Agency and Integrality: Philosophical Themes in the Ancient Discussions of Determinism and Responsibility.* Dordrecht: Reidel, 1987.

[81] Zimmerman, Michael. "Moral Responsibility, Freedom, and Alternate Possibilities." *Pacific Philosophical Quarterly* 63 (July 1982): 243–54.

INDEX

Ability: impotence toward future, 7–8, 9, 13; and language-learning, 16; as necessary to performance of act, 17; and inductive arguments, 18, 65; to change past, 66, 67; temporal indexing of, 68, 69–71, 73, 74, 96–98, 105, 106; gain and loss of, 107, 108–9; regarding PAP and "'ought' implies 'can'," 113, 114, 116, 118, 119, 129

Analyzing, 80; as distinguished from stipulating, 81, 83–85, 87, 111; of responsibility statements, 133

Antifatalism, 2, 6, 8; allied with metaphysical fatalist, 12, 13, 17, 19, 20; and counterfactuals, 25, 45, 49–50, 53, 57–59, 96

Aristotle, 1; definition of truth, 35, 37, 38, 67, 145–46 n.1, 151–52

Armstrong, B., 149 n.1

Articulating. See Analyzing

Austin, J. L., 148 n.9

Ayer, A. J., 47–48

Backward causation. See Retro-causation

Beer, M., 152

Berkeley, G: and Master Argument, 13, 80; as self-proclaimed descriptivist, 81–84, 87

Bernstein, M., 151–52, 154

Black, M., 153

Blumenfeld, D.: and PAP, 99–102

Bramhall, J., 79

Causality, 21; as related to fatalism, 26, 27–28; transivity, 32, 52, 59; and changing the past, 69; and 'can', 92; and moral responsibility, 122–23, 124, 137, 152, 153

Causal loop, 32

Causation. See Causality

Changing the past, 7, 8, 12; as part of logical fatalism, 13; as understood by metaphysical fatalism, 14; and retro-causation, 30, 57–59, 65; and impossibility, 66, 67–68; and Lewis, 69, 71–72, 75–77,

Changing the past (*cont.*)
113–15; regarding "'ought' implies 'can'," 118, 123

Clarifying. *See* Causality

Closed past, 7–9, 11–13, 69

Compatibilism, 27; and logical fatalism, 28–29; of free will and determinism, 61, 77–78; and Hume, 80, 85–87; using conditionalism, 92, 93, 95; and moral responsibility, 113; and Wittgenstein, 127–43, 149 n.4

Counterfactuals: defined, 21; assessed, 22, 23–25, 28, 29; in account of retrocausation, 30–31; and PAP, 98–100, 152

Counterfatalism. *See* Antifatalism

Deductive arguments, 17, 18

Deliberation, 120; and past actions, 121–22, 140; if possible with knowledge, 141, 142, 149 n.3

Dennett, D., 33

Determinateness, 74–75

Determinism, 3, 26; as term of art, 61, 62; definition of, 63, 64–65, 68; and Lewis, 69, 70, 78; compatibility with free will, 79, 80, 84; formulations of, 85, 86–87, 92, 96; and moral responsibility, 120, 124, 128–43; and Wittgenstein's fatalism, 147 n.1, 149 n.4, 153

Donnellan, K., 148 n.5, 148 n.1, 151

Driver, J., 103

Elucidating. *See* Analyzing

Eternal, 42–43

Facts: and RT, 37, 38; tensed, 39; tensing of, 43–47, 48–51, 53

Fischer, J. M., 153

Fleming, N., 149 n.1

Flew, A., 153

Forgie, W., 149 n.1

Frankfurt, H., 98, 99, 101; and PAP, 102, 153, 154

Free will, 3, 33, 61, 77, 78; compatibility with determinism, 79, 80, 85; ordinary use of, 86, 87, 88; van Inwagen's account, 91, 92, 95; and volitional view, 124; Wittgenstein's view, 127–43

Gale, R., 152

Goodman, N., 152

Gravity: as compelling force, 131–32

Grice, H. P., 151

Grünbaum, A., 146 n.5

Halpin, J., 152

Heisenberg, W., 36

Hobbes, T., 79

Horwich, P., 151, 153

Hume, D.: analysis of causation, 27, 29; view of free will, 80, 86–88, 123; skepticism, 137–38, 152

Inductive arguments, 18

Kidney analogy, 134–35; analogue to human freedom, 135–36, 143

Kripke, S., 148 n.5, 148 n.1, 151

Law of excluded middle (LEM), 36–37, 45–46; tensed, 57, 59

Lewis, D.: changing the past, 68–

70; moral responsibility, 113–20, 123–24, 145n.3, 147n.8, 148n.1, 152

Locke, D., 153

Logical fatalism, 2; defined, 6, 7–8, 10; distinguished from metaphysical fatalism and antifatalism, 12–13; related to Master Argument, 14–16, 18; and validity, 19; and counterfactuals, 22–24; and causality, 26–29, 62; connection with determinism, 64, 95; and moral responsibility, 111, 125

McCall, S., 147n.6, 147n.9

MacKenzie, J. S., 43

Mackie, J., 152

McTaggart, J. M., 36, 145n.1

Martinich, A. P., 104, 109, 149n.2

Master Argument, 13–15

Maugham, Somerset, 24

Mellor, D. H., 152, 153

Meta-ability, 106–7; gain of, 108; as method to resolve Martinich/Sinnott-Armstrong debate, 109

Metaphysical fatalism, 2, 5; explicated, 6, 8, 13, 19; and physical theories, 21; and counterfactuals, 24; and retrocausation, 32–33, 62; relation to determinism, 65; and compatibility problem, 93, 95; and moral responsibility, 111; and PAP, 112, 113, 124, 125. *See also* Past necessity

Metaphysical necessity. *See* Moral responsibility

Moral dilemmas, 110

Moral responsibility, 3, 88, 95; re-

quiring freedom, 96, 97, 101–2, 104; and meta-abilities, 106–7; and moral dilemmas, 110–11; and PAP, 112, 113; toward past events, 114, 115–17; and " 'ought' implies 'can'," 118, 119–25, 128, 129; suppositions of, 133–36; and free choice, 137, 153

Naylor, M., 145n.3, 154

Oaklander, N., 152

Ockhamism, 58, 147n.7

Open future, 7, 12, 40, 69; and our abilities, 73; and determinateness, 75

" 'Ought' implies 'can' " principle, 3, 96, 97; and PAP, 100; rejection of, 104; relationship with meta-abilities, 106–7, 109; and moral dilemmas, 110–11, 112–13; and Lewis, 114, 115, 117, 119; in extended form, 118

Paradigm case arguments, 89; persuasiveness of, 90, 91; greatest plausibility of, 92, 138

Paradox of promising: Driver's articulation of, 103–4; debate between Martinich and Sinnott-Armstrong, 104–9

Parmenides, 36, 53, 145n.1

Passmore, J., 153

Past necessity, 2, 10, 12; related to abilities, 20; and causal relationships, 29–30, 33, 65, 111–12; and moral responsibility, 124

Pears, D., 153

Possible worlds, 4; and counterfactuals, 21–25; and causality, 27;
and tensed truths, 56; in definition of determinism, 63, 64, 84;
and causal necessitation, 124,
147 n.1

Power, 6; and importance toward
future, 9; in definition of logical
fatalism, 10, 11; different senses
for metaphysical and logical fatalism, 12, 13; and Master Argument, 14–16; and retrocausation,
30, 57, 59, 63; in Hume's account
of freedom, 86, 88, 103, 133, 141,
147 n.7

Presuppositions, 2; of fatalists and
antifatalists, 35, 47; of a plausible
fatalism, 59; of anti-paradigm
case arguments, 90

Priest, G., 152

Principle of alternate possibilities
(PAP): statement of, 97; history
of, 98–103, 104, 111–13; and
Lewis, 114, 115–17, 153

Principle of bivalence (PB), 36;
tensed, 57, 146 n.2

Prior, A. N., 152

Propositions: as truth bearers, 35,
36; and facts, 37, 39; tensed, 40;
internal and external references
of, 41, 42–45, 47, 49, 50–51; temporal indexing of, 52, 54–55, 56–
58, 69, 83, 145–46 n.1, 153

Putnam, H., 148 n.5

Quine, W. V., 151–52

Representative fatalism (RF): articulation of argument, 38, 40;

tensed version, 45–46; and Ayer,
48, 59

Restricted thesis of truth (RT), 36,
37; argument for, 38–39; tensing
of, 45, 46, 54; tensed version, 57,
59, 145–46 n.1

Retrocausation: possibility of, 30;
arguments against, 31–32, 58;
and Lewis, 123, 153

Ryle, G., 42

Schwyzer, H., 149 n.1

Sea battle, 38–39, 46, 49, 58, 59

Sinnott-Armstrong, W., 104, 109

Smart, J. J., 159

Smith, Q., 152

Smith, W., 149 n.1

Smythies, Y., 3, 107

Sorabji, R., 151

Spinoza, B., 82

Stalnaker, R., 152

Stipulating, 80; distinguished from
analyzing, 81, 83–85

Strasser, M., 154

Stawson, P., 151

Swineburne, R., 152

Tarski, A., 36, 145–46 n.1

Tautology, 6, 8–9, 14, 20, 111, 132

Taylor, R., 148 n.3, 148 n.7

Temporal theory of propositions
and facts (TTPF), 47, 49

Tense: in definition of logical fatalism, 6, 7, 9; of facts, propositions,
and truths, 39–40, 45–49; and
changeability, 50–56, 57, 59, 63,
71; as applied to existence, 73;
changing as opposed to affecting,
74, 75, 145 n.1, 152–53

Tolman, R. C., 153
Train: as compelled object, 130–32, 138
Truth: in deductive and inductive arguments, 18, 33, 35; and Tarski, 36; as property of propositions, 37, 39; internal and external references of, 41–43, 45–46; tensing of, 47, 48–52; argument for tensed, 53, 54; temporal and atemporal accounts of, 55, 56–57, 71, 82–83, 107

Validity, 18–19, 89, 107; and " 'ought' implies 'can' " principle, 109

Van Inwagen: assessment of fatalism, 44; and changing the past, 68, 86; account of free will, 87, 88–89; and paradigm case arguments, 90, 91–92, 146n.3, 148n.1, 149n.3, 153
Verbal issue, 2, 20, 24; of tensed propositions, 57, 79, 97, 111, 149n.3

White, M., 4, 151
Wilkins, B., 149n.1
Wittgenstein, L., 3, 22, 41, 127–43

Zimmerman, M., 153